BUILDING A ROMAN
LEGIONARY FORTRESS

ELIZABETH SHIRLEY

First published 2001

PUBLISHED IN THE UNITED KINGDOM BY:

Tempus Publishing Ltd
The Mill, Brimscombe Port
Stroud, Gloucestershire GL5 2QG

PUBLISHED IN THE UNITED STATES OF AMERICA BY:

Arcadia Publishing Inc.
A division of Tempus Publishing Inc.
2 Cumberland Street
Charleston, SC 29401
1-888-313-2665

Tempus books are available in France, Germany and Belgium
from the following addresses:

Tempus Publishing Group	Tempus Publishing Group	Tempus Publishing Group
21 Avenue de la République	Gustav-Adolf-Straße 3	Place de L'Alma 4/5
37300 Joué-lès-Tours	99084 Erfurt	1200 Brussels
FRANCE	GERMANY	BELGIUM

British Library Cataloguing in Publication Data.
A catalogue record for this book is available from the British Library.

ISBN 0 7524 1911 0

Typesetting and origination by Tempus Publishing.
PRINTED AND BOUND IN GREAT BRITAIN

Contents

List of illustrations, tables and notes

Text figures

Tables

Notes

Preface and acknowledgments

This book describes, from a practical viewpoint, how Roman legionary fortresses might have been planned for and built, and how they might have looked and performed. It includes an examination of their structural design and the techniques used, calculation of the type and amount of building materials and equipment needed, and their supply. The type and amount of labour needed is assessed and discussed, together with its supply and support, the sequence of work, its organisation, and the construction period.

Based on a wide variety of sources, this book emphasises the practical aspects of planning for, constructing and maintaining fortress buildings and features. Roman fortresses are considered not as architectural features or symbols of Roman might, but as complexes built by soldier-workmen from basic materials, often in adverse conditions and in remote areas. Establishing the likely nature and quantities of these building materials, equipment and labour allows a detailed examination of the resource implications of building a fortress. This is particularly useful when considering the practicalities of a military advance. It also gives some insight into the day-to-day life of legionaries, their range of practical and organisational skills, and the effects of the presence of the Roman army on a region.

Chapter 2 outlines Roman building technology, the scope and sequence of supply and construction work, and the appearance of and conditions in a fortress. Chapter 3 describes the initial construction work, including clearing the site, setting-out, and constructing the defences and any extramural features. Chapters 4 and 5 describe the design and amounts of materials and labour required for the timber and masonry buildings and features, and chapter 6 describes streets, drainage, and water-supply. Chapter 7 discusses the labour required to support and supply the legionaries who carried out the building work. This includes supervision, organisation and administration, welfare, military training and guarding, and the manufacturing/processing/acquiring of materials and equipment. Chapter 8 discusses transport on and to site, and chapter 9 the likely composition and size of the construction-force, work programmes and construction periods.

This book would not have been completed without the support of my husband, Dr Stephen Sangwine, who also turned my sketches into line illustrations. I am also very grateful to Ross Whitlock for his illustrations.

The photographs of Roman tools are reproduced by kind permission of the Museum of London. The photographs of Richmond's Inchtuthil excavations are reproduced by kind permission of the Administrators of the Haverfield Bequest, University of Oxford. Richmond's plan of Inchtuthil from Pitts and St Joseph, 1985, is reproduced by kind permission of the Society for the Promotion of Roman Studies.

Elizabeth Shirley
Reading, September 2000

1 Introduction

How were Roman legionary fortresses built? What tools and materials were needed, how much labour, and how long did it take to complete a fortress? How were the buildings and features designed, and how did they function? How was the building work, and its support and supply, organised? These practical questions about Roman fortresses are explored in this book.

Most of the remains we have of Roman legionary fortresses are of masonry, but it is probable that all fortresses were built initially in timber, with turf ramparts. This is because, as is shown here, a fortress could have been built very much more rapidly in timber, and from building materials that were available locally or manufactured quickly. Rebuilding in masonry could then proceed as rapidly, or as slowly, as demands and resources allowed.

The fortress at Inchtuthil, near Perth in Scotland, was never rebuilt in masonry, and was abandoned before the initial timber-phase was completed. Study of its remains suggests how the timber-phase of any Roman fortress was built, and that even its initial timber-phase included some masonry, mostly in the late stages. Inchtuthil was trench excavated by Richmond in the 1950s and '60s and is the only fortress for which we have a complete plan. This fortress has been studied to calculate the quantities of building materials, tools and equipment, and the various different types of labour required to build any fortress, both the initial timber-phase and the later rebuilding in masonry. These calculations give us insights into the organisational and constructional abilities of the Roman military, and the day-to-day lives of Roman soldiers.

Legionary fortresses and the Roman army

The size and composition of the Roman army varied over time, and is well discussed elsewhere (see Bibliography). The Roman army was divided into legions (elite troops, who were Roman citizens), and auxiliary units, with some irregular units, and the fleet (e.g. *Classis Britannica*). Auxiliary units comprised infantry (*peditata*), cavalry (*ala*) or mixed units (*equitata*) of about 500 (*quingenary*) or 1,000 (*milliary*) men. These were housed in forts (mostly 1-10ha or 2.5-25 acres), of which about 250 are known in Britain. The legions were housed in fortresses of about 20ha (or 50 acres). Sixty-six fortresses are known, of which 10 were in Britain; these were not all extant at the same time (**1 & 2**). There is considerable similarity between fortresses (and between forts) but no two are exactly the same.

Legions and auxiliary units were often below strength, but it is not clear whether their numbers were the fighting or the establishment strength, or how much extra should be

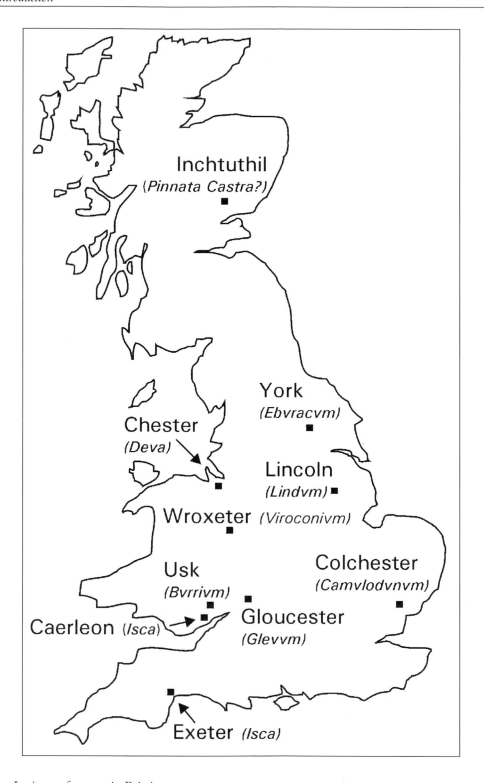

1 Legionary fortresses in Britain

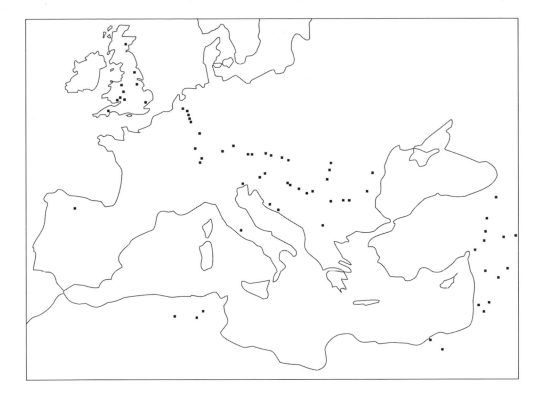

2   Legionary fortresses in mainland Europe

allowed for non-combatants and dependants. The actual size of a legion is likely to have differed between wartime and peacetime conditions, and between the frontier and an established garrison. The exact size of a legion is not known. A legion was divided into 10 cohorts. Cohort I (the elite centuries) had, from the first century AD, five double-centuries (5 x 160 men); cohorts II to X each had six centuries of about 80 men (6 x 80 = 480), plus a probable 120 cavalrymen. This gives a total of about 5,240 (800 + 4,320 + 120) plus the senior officers, say about 5,300 men plus any non-combatants.

The legion was commanded by the *legatus legionis*, a senatorial appointment usually of about 2 or 3 years duration; he was not a career soldier. The second in command was the *tribunus laticlavius*, aided by five junior *tribunes*; their roles were largely administrative. The third in command was the *praefectus castrorum*, a career soldier who was responsible for supply logistics. Each century was commanded by a *centurion*, aided by an *optio*. Within each century there were *principales* (who had specialist roles, e.g. book-keeper) and *immunes* (who were exempt from certain fatigues in recognition of their specialist skills).

The army, though not necessarily every legion, probably had men with the skills necessary for providing everything the army needed. These would range from directly military, logistic and administrative skills, to the direct provision of equipment (e.g. manufacturing weapons), materials (e.g. extracting and processing iron-ore) and foodstuffs (e.g. growing wheat). Legionaries were trained in constructing earthworks and buildings, and legions probably included specialists to manufacture and process building materials. The full range of these skills is not known, but Paternus gives a list of a legion's specialists, and although it may not be complete or accurate for the whole Roman period, it does indicate a wide range of constructional skills. These include surveyors, an architect or engineer, ditch-diggers, glaziers, shinglers/roof-tile makers, conduit-inspectors (water-engineers), plumbers, blacksmiths, masons, lime-burners, and wood-cutters. A legion would have needed only a few men with specialist building skills.

Even when building a new fortress in a hostile region, a legion would have required a considerable amount of equipment; a garrisoned legion probably amassed much more. This all had to be transported, organised and maintained. Each legionary had personal weaponry and equipment, including a short sword (*gladius*), a dagger (*pugio*), and throwing spear (*pilum*), a large shield and protective cover, and perhaps a two-edged sword (*spatha*). Each soldier may also have had a saw, axe, basket, pick, sickle, chain, earthcutter and entrenching tool, though some of these may have been held in common. He also had clothing, body-armour and helmet, and personal effects. Each *contubernia* (group of eight soldiers) would have needed messing equipment, bedding and a tent, and may have had a pack-animal to transport this. There must also have been administrative equipment, medical supplies, and ceremonial clothing and equipment. Legions also had artillery (probably 10 *ballista* per legion, and 55 *catapulta*), horses for the officers and cavalrymen, pack-animals, supply-wagons, and equine equipment. There must also have been a wide range of specialist tools (for building, agriculture or foraging, iron-working etc.), and a supply of food and fodder.

Investigating legionary fortresses

The first step here is the theoretical reconstruction of the buildings, defences and other features. This can be done using the archaeological remains (which are usually limited, especially for the timber phase of a fortress; *see* **3**), analogous sites, Roman and pre-mechanisation builders' 'handbooks', finds, experimental archaeology, and informed pragmatism about the building process. Strictly speaking, 'reconstruction' is an inaccurate term; all that can be suggested is a plausible way of constructing the buildings, consistent with the evidence, with traditional building practice, and with common sense.

Often it is necessary to consider a range of options about building-shape, structural design, construction methods, and materials, but these options must have been available to the Roman army, and they must be functionally realistic. Detailed calculations, based on these varied options, show that the key questions in determining the scale of supply are: the plan-dimensions of the buildings and their three-dimensional sizes and shapes; the general construction method; the materials used, and their dimensions; and Roman work-rates.

3   *Wall trenches at Inchtuthil. The wall trenches of a front wall and partition wall of a building to the north of the* via principalis. Haverfield Bequest

The practicalities of building

Buildings are often seen by archaeologists and historians as manifestations of a material culture, with an emphasis on architectural appearance, socio-political impact, dating, and historical associations. There is also a bias toward the grander, often public buildings, and those built of substantial (and archaeologically durable) materials. However, the simpler fortress buildings (e.g. barracks) are very significant; they needed more materials and labour and occupied more ground than a fortress's principal buildings (e.g. the headquarters building).

It is also important to see fortress buildings as remnants of a practical process (design, supply, construction, and maintenance, and its planning and organisation) and as places where people lived and worked. An understanding of these processes and conditions can tell us a great deal about the abilities, resources, socio-political conditions, values, and day-to-day lives of the people that produced them. The construction process itself, with its associated organisation and supply, was a major element in the economy, and a major achievement in its own right. Establishing the scale of the supply of materials and labour for building a fortress helps to identify whether such construction projects were a major challenge or part of the army's normal activities.

The architectural appearance of the fortress buildings is of course important. It would have affected those who saw them (whether military or civilian, Roman or native) with a variety of impacts (e.g. reassurance; awe; intimidation), and would have been a factor in their design. However, what is often overlooked is what the buildings would have been like to live and work in (were they draughty? damp? dark?), and the interrelationship between their internal environments and the design, construction methods, and materials used.

From the evidence available to us today it is not possible to describe definitively what a fortress looked like or how it was constructed. However, it is possible to describe plausible three-dimensional shapes, basic structural designs, materials, and working methods and conditions. We have no direct evidence about the labour-force, its size, how it was organised, the balance between skilled and less-skilled people, military or civilian, or how these may have varied during the initial construction, or for rebuilding a fortress in masonry. However, by using indirect evidence, it is possible to describe the scope of the tasks, make plausible suggestions, and highlight the complexity of this aspect of construction.

It is implausible that those on site would have been responsible for the entire supply process, particularly during the timber-phase. The on-site organisers could have, for example, estimated the number of nails required, but are unlikely to have been directly involved in extracting and processing the iron-ore from which they were made. They were probably able to draw on iron billets (if not nails) produced or obtained centrally by the army.

The enormous scale of supply necessary to build a fortress does illustrate the administrative and organisational demands on and abilities of the Roman army. It implies considerable control of materials, components and raw materials, over a wide area, and with significant advanced planning. Unless there was either vast wastage due to over-supply, or considerable delays due to under- and/or late-supply, this planning process must have been sophisticated. It would have involved establishing how much (of each type of building material, item of equipment, and labour specialism) would have been needed, and when, and obtaining it and transporting it, at the right time, and in the right quantities. The different lead-in times for obtaining the different materials and components (extracting/processing/manufacturing/purchasing/etc.), and the varying difficulties in their transportation, would have required flexibility and considerable co-ordination. Only some materials (e.g. iron billets) could have been stockpiled against future demand, but this also implies a sophisticated organisational and administrative process.

The importance of the initial (timber) phase

The more complex the remains of a fortress building are, the less 'accurate' the reconstruction is likely to be. With a timber barracks, for example, there are significantly fewer plausible design and materials options than with, say, a masonry *praetorium*. Reconstructions of timber buildings are thus more reliable. They also have another major advantage: the construction period for rebuilding in masonry is much harder to determine than that for the initial timber-phase.

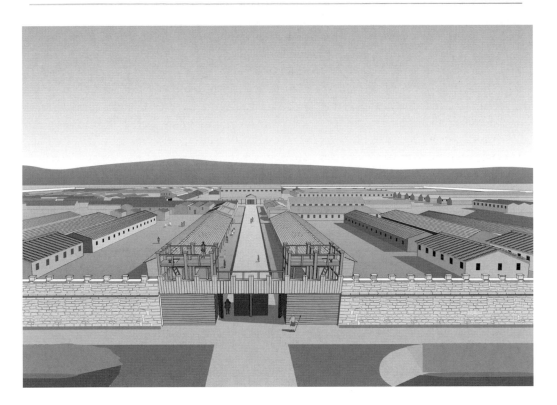

4 *Approaching the main gate. A reconstruction of Inchtuthil at the beginning of the late stage of the timber-phase. The turf-rampart has been rebuilt in stone, but the buildings are of timber. The main street (*via praetoria*) runs from the gate (*porta praetoria*) to the headquarters (*principia), with store buildings either side. There are barracks and centurions' quarters to right and left, and in the far corners. The hospital is in the distance, to the right.* Ross Whitlock

The best known timber-phase fortress is Inchtuthil (**4** & **5**); it also has the most complete ground-plan of any known Roman legionary fortress, and a known site occupancy of less than three years (in the 80s AD). Inchtuthil thus provides a unique opportunity for the study of fortress construction. We know the size and location of all its internal buildings, and can infer their construction. From this, the quantities of building materials, equipment, and labour can be calculated, and the work-programme and labour-force suggested. Thus we can be reasonably sure of the amounts and types of materials, equipment and labour needed to build a fortress, and know something of the planning and organisation required. (See Shirley, 2000, for full details of this reconstruction, assessment of quantities of labour and materials, and discussion.) The construction of the fortress at Inchtuthil must have been similar to the initial phase of construction of any Roman legionary fortress.

Inchtuthil is in Perthshire, Scotland, on the River Tay $9\frac{1}{2}$ miles (15km) from Perth (where the river is tidal) and 7 miles (11km) south of Dunkeld; the valley here is a natural routeway into the Highlands of Scotland. The fortress and extramural features occupy

5   *View from the north-west gateway (*porta dextra*) at Inchtuthil. This view towards the north-east corner shows the houses of the centurions of the first cohort, with barracks to the left of the picture, and store buildings to the right. The* fabrica, *hospital and* principia *are in the distance.*
Ross Whitlock

most of a plateau, about 45m above sea-level, within a widening of the River Tay's alluvial plain. The Tay is likely to have been the main source of water and transport to the fortress. Before it was finished, the fortress at Inchtuthil was systematically demolished, but the stone extramural bathhouse and the stone refacing of the rampart suggest that there was an initial intention of permanence.

The fortress covered nearly 22ha (54 acres; 472 x 460m within the defensive walls), and it was defended by a turf rampart (with later stone facing-wall) ditch and counter-scarp bank. Within the defences are 66 barrack blocks, over 170 store-buildings, a small *principia* (headquarters), a large *fabrica* (workshop) and hospital, four tribunes' houses, six granaries, and an aisled hall (*basilica exercitatoria*). There was a prepared site for a *praetorium* (legate's residence) and main bathhouse, and room for three or four more tribunes' houses and two more granaries; these important but initially less vital buildings, and a larger *principia*, would probably have been built, presumably in masonry, following the completion of the timber buildings. Close by are a probable stores compound, senior officers' residence and bathhouse, and three temporary camps and associated earthworks. These extramural features may be less typical, but some form of temporary accommodation and store areas would have been necessary for building any fortress. There was probably an aqueduct and a parade ground, but no trace has yet been found.

2 Fortress construction, appearance and function

Fortress layout and buildings

There are many features common to Roman fortresses, although there is no 'standard' layout or complement of buildings (e.g. Vetera, in Germany, was a double legionary fortress with two legate's residences; Chester had an elliptical peristyle building). They were defended (but not defensive) sites, usually on or close to communications routes and often near rivers, rectangular in plan-shape (though of differing proportions), with a defended area of approximately 20ha (50 acres) behind an initial turf-rampart with ditch and counter-scarp bank. The layout of the fortress at Inchtuthil is shown in figures **6** and **7**.

A fortress usually had four gateways, with the main street (the *via praetoria*) running from the main gateway (the *porta praetoria*) and meeting, at right-angles, the *via principalis*. The *praetentura* area (between the front-wall and the *via principalis*) housed barracks and stores buildings. The *via decumana* ran from the rear gateway (the *porta decumana*) to the *via quintana*, and the *retentura* area between this and the rear-wall also housed barracks, stores and workshop buildings. The central *latera praetorii* (between the *via principalis* and *via quintana*) housed the more prestigious buildings: the *principia* (headquarters) which faced the front gateway, the *praetorium* (the legate's house), the bathhouse, and the hospital (the *valetudinarium*). Immediately inside the defences and running all the way round the perimeter was another main street (the *via sagularis*), and there would have been minor streets linking the buildings with the main streets.

The *principia*, with its central position and vital function, was a large building, probably designed to be visually impressive. It typically comprised a large hall (*basilica*), with a range of rooms (offices, strongroom, and an *aedes* housing the legion's standard) and a courtyard, usually enclosed by a roofed walkway. The *praetorium*, also a large and impressive building, was designed much as a grand civilian house, and would have had residential, social, and administrative functions. The hospital, usually a range of wards around a central courtyard or garden, was often large enough to accommodate 5-10% of a legion.

The barracks were distributed around the fortress, usually to the front and rear areas. Each cohort had six barrack blocks, aligned parallel to each other, often in facing pairs (**8**). There is considerable variation in the precise numbers and types of buildings in a fortress, and variation in the design, size and proportions of barracks. They were long buildings, rectangular in plan (usually 30-100 x 7-15m) and divided into *contubernia* (usually 10-13 in number), each comprising a front and rear room (probably for storage and sleeping respectively). Most barracks had a covered walkway or verandah along their front elevation. Centurions were housed in individual houses, built close to or attached to their

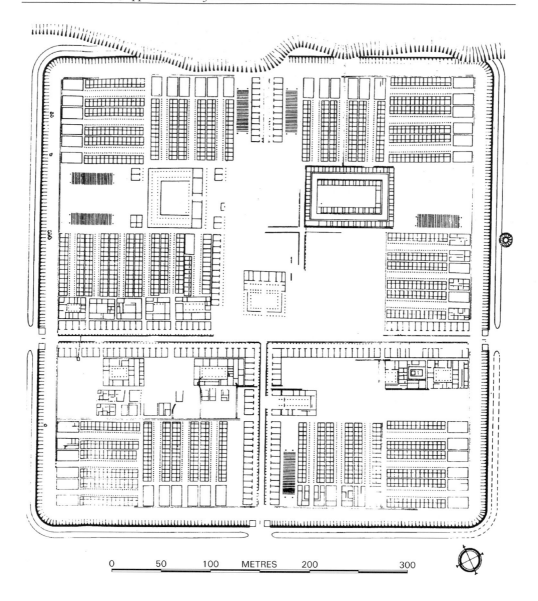

6 *Richmond's plan of Inchtuthil. This is reproduced from Pitts and St Joseph, 1985.* Society for the Promotion of Roman Studies

barrack block. The elite first cohort were usually housed in the *latera praetorii* area, often in barracks a little larger than those of the other cohorts. Their centurions (the legion's most senior centurions, each in charge of a double-century) had larger and grander houses. The tribunes' houses were larger still, and usually reminiscent of the civilian peristyle (a range of rooms around a central courtyard).

The bathhouse, which served the entire legion, would also have been large and impressive. In the initial timber-phase of a fortress it was perhaps the first masonry

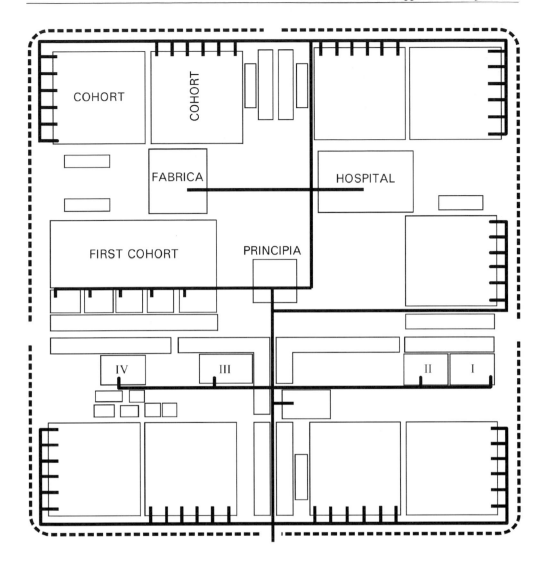

7   *Inchtuthil's main features*

building (all the other buildings could function adequately in timber, but bathhouses had to be of brick or stone). Each fortress had one or more workshops (*fabrica*) for repair or production of weaponry, tools and equipment, and several granaries. These, again, were large buildings, often distributed around the fortress (where they were less vulnerable, and perhaps more accessible). Their entrances were often close to the main streets, presumably to make deliveries easier. Each fortress had a considerable number of store-buildings (*tabernae*), usually long narrow buildings, subdivided into storerooms of various widths, and positioned along the main streets. It is possible that some were offices or specialist workshops; some probably stored the legion's larger and spare weaponry and equipment, tools, non-grain food items, crockery, clothing, etc.

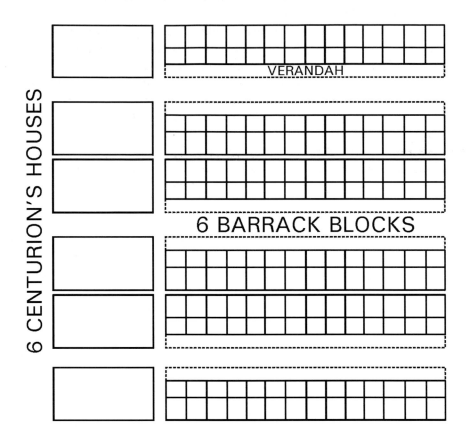

VERANDAH

6 CENTURION'S HOUSES

6 BARRACK BLOCKS

8   A cohort block

Roman building technology and design

Timber structures

Timber structures are affected by a variety of factors (including timber strength; load types, distribution and duration; framing method; the spacing of members; jointing; notching; and the use and maintenance of the building), and are subject to buckling, bending, shear and racking forces. The outline structural designs suggested here allow for these, and for the structural characteristics of timber. Timber strength, for example, is affected by the species of tree, moisture-content, density, natural defects, the angle of the grain, and how it is jointed. Ideally these matters should be explicitly allowed for in the design, but the structural design of Roman buildings could only have been based on trial-and-error, experience, and tradition. Timber structures are essentially simpler than masonry ones, and structural weaknesses, unless severe, are easier to rectify. If a framing weakness becomes evident, or develops due to decay, then additional braces, ties, struts or props can often be added to remedy the weakness.

The shapes, sizes and layouts of military buildings, although not standardised, do exhibit marked similarities, and it is likely that the size, arrangement and spacing of their timbers did too. Where design is based on experience, it is unlikely to result in the most efficient use of materials, particularly if those materials are not in short supply. Much over-sizing in historical buildings is due to a lack of understanding of the structural relevance of cross-sectional shape, with timbers typically both larger and squarer in section than necessary. Roman fortress excavation evidence does show a variety of different cross-sectional shapes, indicating a lack of standardisation in timber shape, and size, and some lack of understanding of its relevance. The timbers in Roman fortresses were probably significantly larger than necessary: traditional timber structures typically have larger timbers, of squarer cross-section and closer spacing than is now known to be structurally necessary.

The practicalities of cutting joints with hand-tools require relatively large timbers. In rough carpentry work about 50mm (2in) is a realistic size for a tenon and the cut-away areas either side, giving a minimum timber cross-sectional size of about 150mm (6in). Also, a mortice-and-tenon cannot perform adequately if it is too small, and there is no reason to assume a shortage of timber. If timber was in short supply, the buildings would probably have included central columns, to reduce roof-spans and thus timber sizes and lengths, or smaller and more closely spaced wall-columns. Generally the use of smaller or shorter timbers requires more complex and/or time-consuming jointing. Speed of construction, presumably an important consideration to the Roman army, favours the use of good quality timber, probably over-sized, rather than spending time on more elaborate framing and jointing methods to produce stable structures from lesser-quality or smaller-section timber.

There is excavation evidence of military wall-framing (e.g. post-and-truss and cill-beams), but no direct evidence for the roof-framing of Roman buildings; the roof spans are the best indicator. Buildings with a rectangular plan are usually roofed with either a gabled roof (with two roof slopes and two gable-end walls above roof level) or a hipped roof, with four roof slopes (*see* **9**). Hipped roofs tend to reduce racking, though at low pitch angles this is not a major concern. The barracks, being long and thin, may have been prone to racking, but this would have been reduced by structural partitions and the aisle-effect of the walkways. Earth-fast foundations (in which timber posts are embedded in the ground) are also effective in reducing racking.

The structural designs suggested in this book are based on excavation evidence, traditional practice (including eighteenth- and nineteenth-century rules-of-thumb and size-tables), and pragmatism. Rules-of-thumb imply that the timber sizes suggested here for Roman fortresses are too small, but traditional size-tables imply that they are larger than necessary! Both assume softwood, at least some mechanical fixings, and much lighter roof-coverings than the Romans had available, all of which need smaller timbers. The theoretical minimum sizes for timbers cannot be calculated because there is virtually no reliable data on the performance of traditional carpentry joints and oak timbers. The general implication is that the timbers would have been larger than structurally necessary.

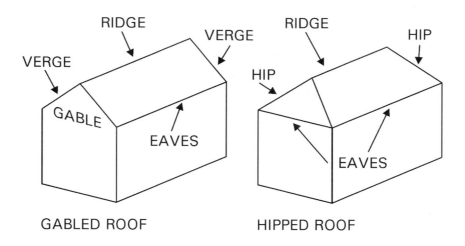

9 Gabled and hipped roofs

The moisture content of timber affects its strength, weight, durability and shrinkage characteristics. Felled timber loses naturally occurring moisture until it reaches equilibrium with the surrounding air; moisture loss increases timber strength and stiffness, but causes shrinkage. The joints are usually the main weakness in a traditional timber structure, and as green timber seasons it gains strength but shrinks, allowing joints to loosen. The moisture content and strength of timber therefore fluctuate with changing climatic conditions (at about 15% moisture content timber is about 40% stronger than when saturated). Fully-seasoned oak is unlikely to have been used because it is very hard to work; the structural timbers would therefore not have reached full strength immediately. As the moisture content of timber reduces, shrinkage and distortion occur; timber-framing is therefore constantly varying slightly in strength.

Another influence on strength is decay. Oak, particularly heartwood, is very resistant to insect infestation, and reasonably resistant to fungal attack. However, timber in prolonged contact with dampness (as opposed to waterlogged conditions) will decay. Oak, though one of the best species for damp conditions (e.g. embedded in the ground, or at roof valleys) would have decayed. Decay causes weakness, and can lead to collapse; routine maintenance and repair would have been necessary to prevent this.

Joints and fixings necessarily reduce the strength of timbers, often at critical points. Some joints are less of a problem than others; some joints are quicker to make than others. There is relatively little archaeological evidence of Roman timber jointing, but it does confirm a range of joints (simple-housings; halvings; saddle-joints; dovetails; mortice-and-tenons; draw-tongue tenons; and dovetail mortice-and-tenons) and that Roman carpenters understood the characteristics of these joints. Nailed joints may have been used, but timber buildings and roofs can be built satisfactorily without nails, using carpentry joints secured with timber pegs.

Masonry structures

There were numerous variations in the construction of Roman masonry walls, but they typically comprised three basic types: homogeneous walls of bonded stone-blocks, concrete walls with brick bonding-courses, and the more common faced walls with outer faces of brick or stone and an inner core of mortar and rubble. The quality of the materials (including the mortar), their preparation, and the workmanship influence performance.

Mortar (sand and lime mixed with water) holds the bricks or stone-blocks together, helps distribute the loads, and reduces weather penetration, but joints must not be too thick. The bricks or stone-blocks are laid with overlapping joints, and the more even this bonding the more even the load distribution, and the less likely parts of the wall are to buckle or settle. The more uniform the size of the bricks/blocks the easier it would have been to obtain good bonding along the wall. A considerable variety of sizes and shapes of bricks and stone-blocks were used. The faces and core would be built up together, with bonding across the wall often improved with large bonding-stones or bonding-courses. Stone-blocks, depending on the workability of the stone and the resources available, may have been of irregular shape, roughly shaped, or regularly shaped and of uniform height (at least within each course).

Stonework or brick-built masonry walls have to be substantial enough to transmit dead, live and wind loads to the ground, and resist the overturning tendencies of vaulting, arches and timber-framed roofs. Masonry walls are subject to vertical and horizontal forces, which can cause structural failure if not controlled by building walls that are stiff enough, and foundations that are wide and deep enough, to resist them. The loads, the design, and the soil conditions are all relevant factors.

Vertical loads on masonry walls can cause crushing, buckling and settling. Crushing can be avoided by increasing wall thickness. Buckling occurs where walls are too thin for their height, and can be avoided by restricting the height of a wall, increasing its thickness, reducing the loading, or by adding buttresses or intersecting walls. Settlement occurs where the soil under the wall is not able to resist the imposed load. Soils vary in strength, and thus the amount by which they consolidate under load, often over short distances. Settlement can be reduced by increasing the width of the foundations, thus distributing the load over a greater area of soil. Masonry walls can also crack or fail due to subsidence (downward movement of the ground), heave (where the soil pushes upwards), spread (where roof rafter-feet are not adequately tied together), or thermal or moisture movements.

Horizontal loads (largely from the soil or wind loading) can cause failure by sliding or overturning. Sliding can be avoided by increasing the weight of the wall, and overturning (by rotation or settlement) by making the wall thicker, or thicker at its base; buttresses also reduce rotation.

Masonry can also fail if loads are not applied at or near the centre of gravity of a wall or column. Masonry is relatively weak in tension, and tension occurs if this eccentric loading is greater than one-sixth of the wall's thickness. Problems can be avoided by reducing the eccentricity or increasing the wall or column thickness. Similarly, arches must be deep enough (from point-of-springing to head) to avoid excessive tension and failure.

Columns can also crush or buckle; much depends on their material, shape, and slenderness (the ratio of height to thickness). The more slender a column is, the less load it can bear and the more likely it is to buckle. Rectangular columns are less efficient than square or circular ones, and columns that are fixed at their tops can support heavier loads than free-standing ones.

Window and door openings, and arches, must be positioned so they do not over-weaken the wall. This means that they must not be too large, nor too close to each other or to the outer edges of the wall. The walling above openings must be supported by horizontal lintels (allowing only relatively narrow openings) or arches. Arches need temporary support (for example by timber centering) until their mortar has hardened.

Roofs

In traditional carpentry the type of roof-framing used depended largely on the span of the roof. King-post trusses were traditionally used for spans of about 6-9m, the size of most of the roof-spans at Inchtuthil. Trussed roofs are thought to be rare in Britain before 1550, though Vitruvius (IV, 2) appears to describe a king-post type truss or a multiple-purlin close-spaced truss. The oldest extant example of this type of roof is the sixth-century roof of St Catherine at Mount Sinai; the truss suggested here is simpler, to allow for rapid and straightforward construction (*see* **23**).

A king-post truss comprises a pair of rafters, tied at their feet by a horizontal tie-beam, with a vertical post (the king-post) between ridge and the tie-beam at mid-span, and angled struts between the base of the king-post and the centre of each principal-rafter. The rafters transfer the roof-load to the wall-framing; the tie-beam prevents the rafters spreading (i.e. pushing the walls outwards); the struts stop the rafters sagging, and the king-post stops the tie-beam sagging. The rafters could have been butt-jointed, or lapped-and-pegged; struts were probably tenoned to rafters, and secured at their bases with notches or chocks. The king-post was probably tenoned to the rafters and tie-beam, and the tie-beam saddle-jointed to the wallplate, or cogged (with no overhang, but more cutting). The critical rafter-to-tie-beam joint could have taken many forms of mortice-and-tenon. The simple truss suggested in this book is preferred to a more complex truss (where principal rafters support purlins and common rafters) because it would have been simpler and quicker to erect.

Trussed roofs traditionally had hipped ends, but gabled roofs are simpler and quicker to erect, and easier to weather. The roofs could, theoretically, have been covered with lead, thatch, timber shingles, or tiles. Lead is unlikely because of its great weight, and the impossible burden it would have imposed on resources. Thatch is unlikely because of the difficulty of supplying sufficient quantities of straw or reed, and the considerable fire risk. Oak shingles are probable, as are clay tiles (*tegulae* and *imbrices*). Tiles are much heavier than shingles, and would have taken much longer to produce and transport. Tiles, largely because of fire risk, were probably used for bathhouses and granaries; with use elsewhere probably for reasons of status, though shingles can be effective and durable. Masonry buildings are likely to have had tiled roofs.

Shingles are thin, flat pieces of timber laid overlapping one another in courses (**10**). Their widths could have varied between about 150-300mm (6-12in), provided they were

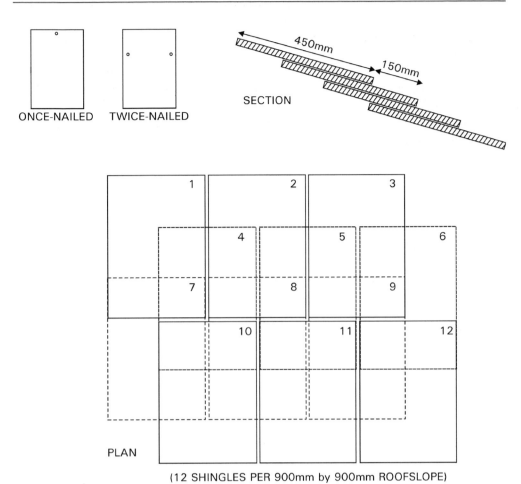

ONCE-NAILED   TWICE-NAILED

450mm

150mm

SECTION

1	2	3
4	5	6
7	8	9
10	11	12

PLAN

(12 SHINGLES PER 900mm by 900mm ROOFSLOPE)

10 Roof shingles

laid with at least 40mm side-lap, but their length (on each course at least) must have been approximately uniform, say a nominal 450mm (18in). A gap (say, 5mm or ¼in) between shingles would have been necessary to allow for moisture movement. Very thin shingles would have been difficult to produce and too prone to splitting, and very thick shingles heavy and harder to fix; a nominal thickness of 10mm is believed likely. The shingles would have been placed, in courses, so that there were always two or three thicknesses of shingle. Treble-thickness would have provided greater insulation and weather-exclusion, but would have been heavier and used more materials.

Tegulae were flat, rectangular tiles with raised flanges on their longer edges, which were laid with their flanges abutting and covered with *imbrices*, which resembled clay pipes cut in half longitudinally (**11**). Evidence from the Beauport Park military tilery (see Brodribb, 1987) suggests the following tile sizes and weights: a nominal *tegula* of 490 x 310 x 20mm (19 x 12 x almost 1in), weighing 6kg (13lb), one-fifth with a single fixing-hole, and *imbrices*

23

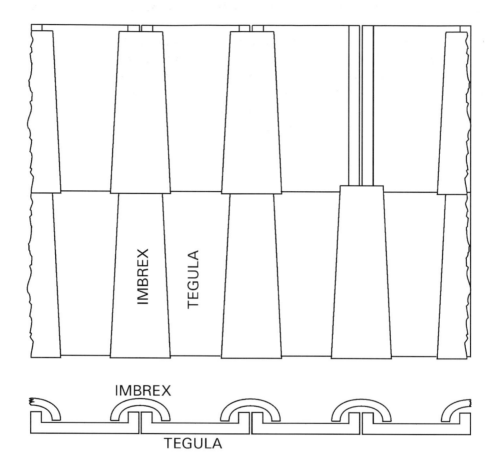

11 Tegulae *and* imbrices

weighing 2.5kg ($5\frac{1}{2}$lb). When laid on a 30° pitched roof there is a loss-to-lap of about 24%, giving a weight of about 86kg (190lb) per m² of roof-slope, plus mortar, fixings, and snow-loading. Double-lapped shingles would have weighed about 21kg (46lb) per m² of roof-slope. Tiles are thus very significantly heavier than shingles, and would have needed a more substantial roof-framing.

Tegulae on roofs over about 30° pitch would have needed fixing to stop them slipping; as most tile finds do not have fixing-holes, Roman roofs probably had relatively low pitches. Tiles were probably fixed to areas vulnerable to wind-damage (e.g. verges, eaves, and areas with exposed aspect). The fixing nails must have been about 60-70mm ($2\frac{1}{2}$in) long and 6mm ($\frac{1}{4}$in) in diameter at the head (such nails were found in a hoard excavated at Inchtuthil). *Imbrices* would have been bedded in mortar (for stability) and pointed (for weather exclusion). All shingles must have had one or two fixings, either nails or oak pegs.

Nails would have been quicker to fix than pegs, but would have involved much greater expenditure of resources.

Masonry vaulted roofs, whether simple barrel or cross-vaults or more complex arrangements, would have exerted considerable outward thrust on their supporting walls, which as a consequence must have been relatively thick to withstand this loading. Vaulted roofs in fortresses probably had tile covering, supported on an outer timber framework. Alternatively, the impression of a vaulted roof could be provided internally, in timber or masonry buildings, by timber-framing and plaster finishes within a gabled or hipped roof.

Flooring

Flooring in timber buildings may have been initially very basic, with a more substantial surfacing installed after occupation. Different timber flooring options are shown in figure **12**. Rammed earth (with some levelling and patching) is the simplest option. It would have required regular repair, and would not have been suitable for all buildings, but may have been an initial finish. Other finishes (including gravel or rammed stone-chippings) imply a raised floor level, with restraining thresholds at doorways. More substantial flooring, likely in the more prestigious timber-phase buildings and in most masonry buildings, include concrete with crushed tile (*opus signinum*) or tessellated brick, stone flags, and mosaics.

Any timber floorboards laid directly onto the ground would have been uneven and insecure, and would have decayed rapidly. Boards (say 25-50mm thick, or 1-2in) were therefore probably fixed to heavy joists (say 100-150mm, or 4-6in square at 1.5-3m spacings) or to joists and bearers.

Underfloor heating was provided by hypocausts, typically in the warm (*tepidarium*) and hot (*caldarium*) rooms of bathhouses and in some principal rooms in some officers' residences. Hypocausts typically comprised a raised floor of large bricks (*bipedales*) supported on columns (*pilae*) of smaller bricks (*bessales*). This underfloor void, about a metre high, was heated by hot gases from the nearby furnace.

Wall treatments and finishes

Rooms with hypocausts often had a void between the wall-structure and its internal finish. These were formed by *tegulae mammatae* (flat tiles, with flanges or spacers, as found at Usk) or box-tiles (*tubulus*, as found at Exeter and Saalburg, about 300mm (12in) wide, 150-450mm (6-18in) high and 85-280mm (3-11in) deep, resembling square-section pipes), fixed with mortar and iron cramps or nails. These voids allowed the hot gases to flow around the walls, and with warm walls the furnaces could operate at lower temperatures. Roof-vaulting in these rooms could be built from hollow voussoir-bricks, allowing all surfaces to be warm.

The walls of timber-framed buildings would have been clad and/or infilled (e.g. with wattle-and-daub) and may have been finished with external and/or internal render. External cladding probably comprised horizontal planks (perhaps with waney edges, and placed with the lower edge lapped over the upper edge of the plank below) fixed with nails or oak pegs. The inner faces of these walls may also have been clad (i.e. forming a cavity, which could also have been infilled). Alternatively, there may have been external cladding

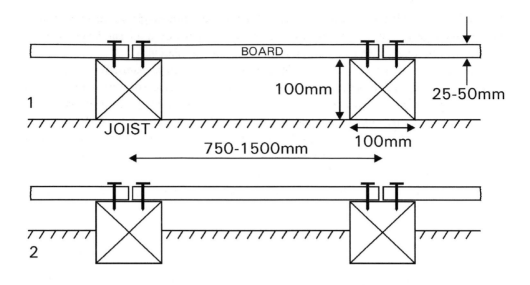

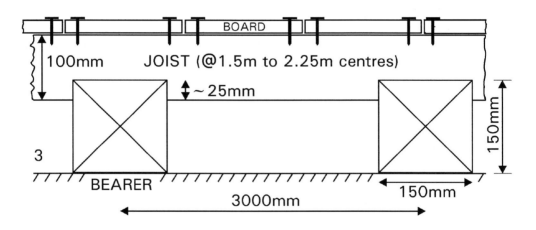

12 Details of timber flooring

and internal infill; or infill to external and internal faces; or infill to the external faces only. Similarly there are various plausible combinations for internal walls. Treatments to internal faces may have been applied later than those to the external face, and not all buildings need have been treated in the same way.

Cladding would have added some rigidity to the walls, and would have been more resistant to decay than wattle-and-daub. It would, however, have required a lot of fixings, which, if nails, would have had very significant resource implications.

There may have been internal finishes in timber-phase fortress buildings. Their presence, and their type and quality, probably varied with the use of the buildings and the status of the occupier. (The presence of at least some window-glass and hypocausts at Inchtuthil suggests that at least some accommodation was not at a basic level.) It is also possible that there was external decoration, but this is speculative.

Masonry walls could have been finished, internally as well as externally, with fair-face work (i.e. no applied finish), but most were probably rendered. Vitruvius describes render-finishes of varying qualities, including nine-coat work incorporating marble dust in the outer coat. The number of coats required would have depended on the roughness of the masonry and the quality (smoothness) of the finish desired. For masonry barracks three-coat work is perhaps the most likely. This render would, in most buildings, probably have been finished with paint, either a plain colour-wash or wall-painting. Not all of this work need have been carried out by soldiers, and the type and quality of the work probably varied with the status of the building.

Lighting, ventilation and access

We do not know the size, shape, position, or the number of window openings, or how many were glazed or had shutters. (One fragment of window-glass was found at Inchtuthil, suggesting either that few windows were glazed or that window-glass was very carefully removed when the fortress was demolished.) For normal daytime use, natural lighting would presumably have been preferred to oil-lamps or candles. Windows, or window-openings, would have provided natural lighting, but at the expense of draughts (even if glazed) and significant labour inputs (i.e. to produce glass, grilles, shutters, etc.). The amount of natural lighting required would have varied depending on the function of the room, and the size, and particularly the depth of the room. Office areas presumably required more lighting than storage areas, but living accommodation is more difficult to assess. Each room probably had at least one window, except where door-openings provided enough lighting (e.g. storage areas?). Clerestory lighting would have maximised natural lighting, particularly for deep rooms and those with walkways.

The alignment of the buildings within fortresses shows that they were not positioned to maximise natural lighting (though this could not have been done without significantly increasing the size of a fortress). The proximity of the buildings to each other (particularly barracks) significantly reduced natural lighting.

Windows in timber buildings were probably the width of the wall-post spacings and perhaps twice as high (about 1100mm or 43in; 350mm or 14in for clerestory windows) (**13**). These sizes are tentative, but do give some indication of the likely number of windows. For example, the dining-room in Inchtuthil's tribune's house I could have had five windows at 550 x 1100mm (22 x 43in) and five clerestory windows at 550 x 350mm (22 x 14in), giving a window-to-floor-area ratio close to modern standards. Alternatively the main external wall may have only had clerestory windows (reducing the window area, but increasing privacy and the quality of the light per unit area), or there might have been windows to give a view of the courtyard. Barracks are a different case though. Some fortresses had blocks built back-to-back with no external wall to the rear rooms, so natural lighting would have been very limited. However, if these rooms were primarily only for sleeping, or use after dark, this might not have mattered, though some ventilation would presumably have been needed.

27

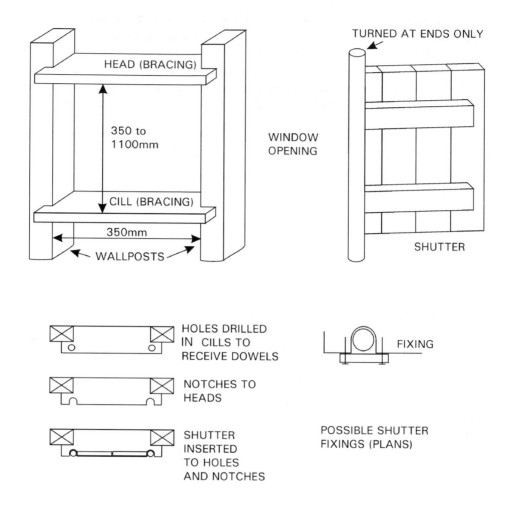

13 Details of windows to timber buildings

In masonry buildings windows were probably relatively small for structural reasons. The limited evidence from excavations of Roman buildings confirms this, and suggests they were at relatively high level.

Every room must have had a doorway (normally located roughly central in the run of wall), but doors might only have been provided where necessary for weather exclusion, heat retention, to enclose odours (e.g. kitchens, latrines), or afford privacy. Thus we cannot assume an internal door for each room. Alternatively some rooms, particularly those not accessible from a corridor, might have had more than one door. There are many plausible positions for doorways, and little evidence. There is some evidence to suggest a rule of thumb for door height to width ratio, though size was presumably related to function.

An external door was perhaps 2m high and 0.8m wide, though internal doors might have been smaller, and main entrance doors larger or arranged in pairs. Doors to granaries, and some workshop and store-buildings were probably larger. The principal buildings (e.g. *principia*, *praetorium*) probably had larger main-entrance doors. Most doors were probably some variant of a ledged-and-braced door, with framing to the larger doors to stop them sagging. They were probably hung with iron hinges, or wooden or iron pivots.

The sequence and scope of the building work

For this analysis, the construction tasks were broken down into various phases. These represent a convenient and logical way of identifying all the tasks, and although not necessarily sequential, probably do indicate the sequence used by the Roman builders. These phases are: extramural preparation (including any temporary camps); pre-construction work (site-clearance, levelling, defences, etc.); assemblage of building materials; surfacing, drainage, and water-supply; building the initial timber and masonry structures; and the later phase of site abandonment or rebuilding in masonry. Clearly some tasks must precede others, but there is no way of establishing the actual sequence of operations. A simplified programme can, however, be suggested. In practice any programme would have been varied to suit variations in the labour supply, availability of materials, the weather and season, and any military influences.

To allow these calculations to be made, each individual construction task, and the number of repetitions, was identified on a building-by-building basis, and a work-rate assessed for each task, together with the likely size of the work-teams. Work-rates assume all-day working and non-extreme conditions, and are based on experimental archaeology, ethnography, pre-mechanisation estimators' handbooks, and common sense. This produced the labour requirements (in man-hours) for each building, and the balance between skilled and less-skilled labour. The labour involved in obtaining the materials and equipment, transporting it to site, and all the organisation, administration, and supervision involved must also be considered.

For most tasks (e.g. roof-truss tie-beams) the calculations involve consideration of four separate stages: collection (i.e. moving the tie-beam timber from the stores to the building); preparation (it is assumed that the timber was cut to the correct cross-section and approximate length before being moved, but that joints were cut on-site); placing (i.e. moving the tie-beam from the site preparation point to its installation location, mostly a lifting task); and fixing (i.e. securing it in place over the wallplates). The calculations identify the minimum numbers of men and man-hours needed for each of these four stages, for each task for each building. Dividing the tasks into these four stages allows the significance of variations to the assumptions to be assessed.

A key matter, largely for the collect stage, is the weight a man could carry over a reasonable distance. This has been assessed at 50kg or 110lb (though one could argue for a higher or a lower figure) but it would of course have varied depending on the nature of the material (principally shape and bulk), the distance, the terrain, and the weather. The suggested sizes of most materials is nominal (e.g. most wall-posts are assumed at 200 x

150mm, or 8 x 6in, with few different lengths needed). Such convenient sizing is perhaps unlikely, but small variations would not have significantly affected labour inputs. (For example, a 3.25m long wall-post would have weighed about 100kg (220lb) and been carried by two men; if it were, say, 150 x 150mm, about 75kg (6 x 6in, and 165lb), it would still have needed two men to carry it.)

Calculating only the total man-hours would be misleading because the number of men for a given task is also relevant. It would also be meaningless to calculate the total man-hours for a building (say 7,000) and then suggest that it took 700 men one day to build it (or one man 700 days), or even a more plausible sounding 70 men 10 days. Some tasks (such as moving a heavy tie-beam) would have required a large team (say 10 or 12 men) while others could not have been done by a large team, and others would be most efficiently done by a small team (e.g. a carpenter and his assistant) or by a series of small teams. Thus team size is specific to the task, not the building.

Some tasks could not have been carried out by individuals, and others would have been more efficiently carried out by teams that balanced skilled and less-skilled men. (Turf-work could most efficiently have been carried out by teams of 12.) Inevitably not all tasks would have been of the same intensity of effort, and in some cases there might have been considerable time wasted waiting for others. (For example, if a lifting team of 12 men misjudged the time a tie-beam would be ready for lifting by only five minutes, a whole man-hour would have been wasted.) There is also the problem of motivation, team-spirit, and shirking to be considered. A legionary was probably well disciplined and supervised, but work may not have progressed as fast as possible if, for example, the soldiers perceived the construction work as routine or non-urgent.

The sequence of operations in fortress construction

Phase One (extramural preparation) is the construction work outside the fortress area, principally setting-out and surfacing temporary camps and storage areas, site-clearance, constructing and later levelling of ditches and banks, and roads. At Inchtuthil this work was carried out in at least three stages, which has implications for team-sizes and the size of the labour-force over time. Phase Two at Inchtuthil was building the officers' temporary camp. This extramural phase may not have occurred at other fortresses.

Phase Three (pre-construction work) includes initial setting-out (defences, main building areas, gateways and the streets), site-clearance (trees and undergrowth from the fortress and surrounding area), any necessary levelling, and the defences. Not all of this need have occurred before the buildings were begun. For the ditch and counter-scarp bank, turfs had to be cut, lifted, transported and placed, the ditch excavated, and the spoil basketed-up, transported and tipped, and the ditch and bank rammed and shaped, and a channel cut in the ditch. The rampart inner-retaining wall involved digging the foundation trench and removing the spoil, collecting, preparing and placing the timbers, and backfilling. For the rampart itself turfs had to be cut and loaded, transported, unloaded and placed, soil had to be dug and basketed-up, transported and placed, and the whole rammed, shaped and turfed. The timbers for the parapet of the ramparts, the walkway and access steps had to be collected, prepared, placed and fixed. The timbers for the four gateways (main uprights; walkways; lookout platforms; parapets and guardrails;

guardrooms; and gates) had to be collected, prepared, placed (including digging foundation post-pits) and fixed.

Phase Four is the assemblage of materials. Timber had to be located, selected and felled, handled (including removing branches and bark), processed (including cleaving or sawing), and perhaps partially seasoned and temporarily stored, and transported. All the stages in bringing the extracted and processed materials (e.g. stone; clay; gravel; lime; mortar admixtures) and manufactured materials (e.g. nails; tiles; glass) must be considered. Similarly for producing and transporting tools and equipment (e.g. scaffolding; ladders; baskets; ropes; cranes; trestles); specialist equipment; transport equipment and draught- and pack-animals; horses; and military, domestic and personal goods, welfare items and food and fodder. Much of this work probably occurred close to the fortress, but some may have come from military stockpiles which predated the decision to build.

Phase Five includes construction tasks other than the buildings themselves: surfacing streets, open-spaces, and courtyards; and drainage and water-supply (culverts; channels, pipework; tanks; latrines). Phase Six is the construction of the timber buildings. Phase Seven is the construction of the few masonry structures built in the initial phase of the fortress. The extent of these is likely to have varied from fortress to fortress; at Inchtuthil they comprised ovens, an extramural small bathhouse, refacing the turf rampart in stone, and presumably the main bathhouse, *praetorium* and enlarged *principia* would probably have been built once the timber buildings were finished.

Phase Eight is either the abandonment of the fortress or its rebuilding in masonry. Once the initial masonry buildings were built, the timing of the rebuilding of the timber buildings is not clear. They could have functioned satisfactorily for many years. Rebuilding could have been a major task over a short period (inevitably several years) or a planned long-term programme, perhaps accounting for much of the legion's activity during the non-campaigning season over many years. A detailed list of these phases for Inchtuthil is given in **Note I**.

Calculating amounts of materials and labour

The key factors influencing the quantities of materials needed are the use of standard units of measurement, eaves-heights, roof-pitch and roof-shape. A detailed consideration of tribune's house I at Inchtuthil identified the critical factors in the design and construction of timber fortress buildings. The calculations for the other buildings were based on the simplest plausible constructional options, but the significance of other options was readily seen. Calculating the labour required to build a fortress follows from these outline designs, the likely building methods (based largely on traditional and current practice, common-sense and intuition, and the limited direct evidence), and an assessment of likely Roman work-rates. An allowance must also be made for the on-site non-constructional labour.

Key factors in determining quantities of materials
There is some evidence for the use of standard units in military planning (usually five Roman feet: 1.48m or almost 5ft), but the evidence is inconclusive. There is no evidence

that standard units were used at Inchtuthil, for example.

The minimum eaves-height of fortress buildings, particularly in the timber phase, was probably related to the average height of a legionary, say 1.80 or 1.75m. Allowing for any rise at the door-threshold (say 200mm, or 8in), clearance at the lintel (say 150mm, or 6in), any walling between lintel and wallplate (say 150mm), and the wallplate itself (150mm), suggests a plausible minimum height of about 2.5m; it could be lower (1.5 standard-units is 2.25m, and two is 2.96m, both of which are also plausible).

Plausible maximum heights are more difficult to estimate. Vitruvius (VI.iii.8.) and Faventinius (XV) give rules-of-thumb for calculating room height based on proportions of room length and breadth. On this basis the principal rooms in Inchtuthil's timber-built Tribunes' Houses would have been an implausible 8m high, 5.5m higher than functionally necessary. If these timber buildings had no ceilings, they would have had floor-to-ridge heights of about 6.3m, giving a more familiar room height and economizing on construction time, labour and materials. Eight metres, though, is quite plausible for masonry buildings constructed in non-urgent circumstances.

A detailed examination of several different design options for tribunes' house I at Inchtuthil (**14**) showed which design options are critical and which are not: the first consideration is the roof design. The rise of a roof (the vertical distance between eaves and ridge) is necessarily determined by the roof-span (the horizontal distance between the eaves) and the roof-pitch (the angle of the roof slope). Roof-span can be taken from the ground-plans (once the roof arrangement and precise wall position has been assessed), and the minimum pitch from that necessary for the roof-covering to be effective (the pitches may have been steeper). The steeper the pitch, the more roof-framing and wall-timbers are needed, and there is necessarily a greater roof-rise. (With a span of 8m, for example, the rise at 30° is 2.3m; at 45° it is 4m.)

Roofs must resist wind pressure and suction, but these are only a significant problem at low (below about 15°) and steep (over 45°) pitches. The minimum effective pitch for oak shingles is 30°, and for tiles 20°; both could have been steeper (up to 45° for shingles and 40° for tiles).

The wings of many courtyard-style fortress buildings are of different widths. At a constant roof-pitch, this would mean each wing had a different roof-rise, with each ridge at a different height. Varying the pitch slightly to give equal ridge-height is not a trivial matter constructionally, and it is therefore more likely that each wing had a simple gabled roof, at least during the timber-phase.

Roof-shape (in practice a choice between hipped- or gabled-roofs) also influences the quantities of materials needed. Hipped-roofs require less walling (i.e. no gable-ends) and have valleys and hips which need weather-protection. Gabled-roofs are quicker and easier to build than hipped-roofs, require less framing and covering, and are easier to weather. Roof-shape was probably determined by balancing various criteria: simplicity (easier and quicker to design and construct), economy (of materials, or of skilled labour), performance (valleys are difficult to weather effectively), and aesthetic considerations (what would look right; what would indicate status or function?). The range of options is enormous; for timber-phase buildings the simpler and more buildable roof options are the more likely.

Eaves-overhangs, if there were any, would have increased the quantities of materials

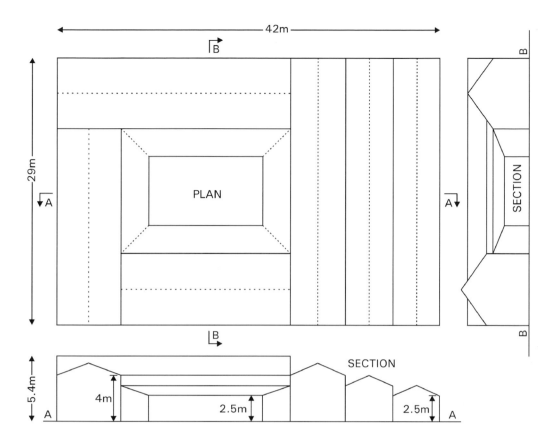

14 Tribune's house I at Inchtuthil

(mostly roof coverings) and labour needed. There is some evidence for eaves-drip channels, suggesting eaves-overhangs or tiles projecting beyond the roof-framing, but it is inconclusive. Eaves-level gutters are unlikely. The degree of any overhang is not known; 150mm might have been adequate to direct run-off away from the walls, but 300mm would have been more effective.

Except for the simplest-shaped buildings, there is no roof arrangement that avoids slopes abutting. These valleys would have been difficult to weather effectively, though water ingress could have been reduced with mortar, and perhaps inverted *imbrices*. Hips and ridges are also difficult to weather, but are less critical because run-off is not concentrated at them. Valleys, hips and ridges would have needed regular maintenance.

The choice of materials used can influence the quantities needed, because physical or performance qualities can influence design. For example, a tiled roof is likely to have a shallower pitch than a shingled roof. The steeper the pitch the greater the roof-slope area, and thus the more roof-covering material used. Also, for the same covering, steeper-pitched roofs usually require more roof-framing timbers, and exert more thrust on the walls, which consequently also have to be thicker. Choice of wall-covering materials (e.g.

cladding, wattle-and-daub, or both, and single- or double-skin?) is also an important influence on quantities.

With masonry buildings, the wall heights and thicknesses and the roofing arrangements are clearly a major determinant of quantities of materials required. Wall height cannot be conclusively determined from foundation and lower-course evidence, but most buildings were probably higher than in the timber-phase, perhaps following Vitruvius' rule-of-thumb, modified by roof-rise and natural lighting influences. There is evidence from extant Roman walls to confirm that walls of substantial height diminished in thickness with height. Masonry buildings would have had timber-framed or masonry-vaulted roofs, probably with tile covering.

Key factors in determining quantities of labour

The detailed assessment of the scale of the effort involved in building a fortress has two main facets: the quantity of materials needed, and the amount of labour required. The latter is based on the former, and on an assessment of likely work-rates, and is thus more tenuous. Also, it is difficult to isolate building a fortress from a legion's other tasks. For example, the legion would have needed food and fodder wherever and whatever it was doing, but the construction might have affected the types of foodstuffs required and the labour needed provide it.

Three main types of labour would have been needed: that for on-site construction work (i.e. those directly engaged in building work), the labour required on-site to directly support those men (e.g. welfare; producing building materials; local transport; and military tasks), and those off-site (e.g. transporting supplies to the site area; producing food, fodder, and specialist materials). The on-site labour can be assessed by detailed calculations, based on isolating each building task and assessing the likely time and team-size involved. The different types of additional on-site labour can be identified, and assessed on an approximate basis; this puts the on-site labour figures into context. The off-site labour can be outlined, but is too tenuous to calculate.

Conditions in a fortress

The internal environments of the fortress buildings would have been influenced by a number of factors, some of which can be suggested with reasonable confidence (e.g. building size and shape). Some factors though are highly conjectural, but of critical influence (e.g. the number, size and positioning of doors, vents and windows).

Fortress timber-framed buildings could have performed to standards which would be regarded as satisfactory today. The main considerations are exclusion of moisture (penetration of rain, snow and dew; condensation; and rising damp), draughts, and heat loss. Wind damage could have been significantly reduced by nailing *tegulae* at verges and eaves, and double-nailing shingles. Rain and snow penetration at valleys need not have been serious providing mortar fillets were well maintained, and heavy snow cleared from roofs. Significant water ingress would only have been likely during prolonged rainfall or very heavy downpours. Heavy driving rain might penetrate a tiled or shingled roof, and so might driven powdery snow, but major problems are unlikely in normal weather conditions, providing roofs were well maintained, and had been built to a reasonable standard. Similarly wall-cladding could have allowed some ingress of driven powdery snow or heavy driven rain, but only in exceptional weather conditions. Shingles and wall treatments would have absorbed moisture (from the air as well as rainfall) but this would have been accommodated within the normal moisture fluctuations of the timber. It might have been a problem in periods of prolonged damp weather, or to any painted wall-plaster.

Exclusion of draughts would have depended on effective sealing of gaps between the components. Two layers of shingles and the closeboarding, if well fitted, should have been relatively draught free. Well-bedded *tegulae* and *imbrices* would have had few air gaps, but would have provided less insulation than shingles. However, the rooms were probably so cold that this would not have made any noticeable difference. Timber wall-cladding would have been draughty, and this in itself is enough reason to argue for the presence of an additional wall treatment (e.g. cladding fixed to the internal face, and/or wattle-and-daub). Wattle-and-daub on its own would have excluded wind, though gaps between it and the framing would have occurred (and needed re-filling) as the timber warped.

Fortress buildings are likely to have been cold, except those with hypocausted rooms (very rare in timber-framed buildings, though Inchtuthil had two). Shelter from the wind will have eliminated wind-chill, but had little effect on temperatures. The rooms were probably draughty, even where windows were glazed or had tightly fitting shutters. Solar gain (i.e. heating from the sun) will have been relatively insignificant, and the buildings were not aligned to maximise it.

Air quality would have been good (because of the draughts) except when braziers or other fires were used. These will have produced carbon monoxide gases (potentially fatal in poorly ventilated rooms), and the smoke and odour must have been unpleasant. Oil-lamps too must have given off odour and smoke, though to a much lesser extent. We do not know how heating and cooking were managed, or which areas were heated, though it seems reasonable to assume that relatively few areas would have been heated on a regular basis. A balance between the advantages and disadvantages of heating and ventilation must have been difficult to achieve.

Timber-framed buildings would have had a life-expectancy equal to that of their framing; the wall-post bases were the most vulnerable area. Oak in direct contact with the ground usually has a life expectancy of about 15-25 years; where fortresses survived that long they were probably rebuilt in masonry before the wall-posts were seriously decayed.

Masonry walls would have needed maintenance too. Structurally sound masonry is subject to surface erosion, and damage from frost, organisms, and thermal and moisture movement. Some movement-induced cracking is likely, requiring remedial work to prevent further decay.

Masonry buildings may have been colder and damper than timber ones, except where heated by hypocausts. Masonry is porous, and thus prone to damp penetration (though this is rarely a major concern with thick walls). Rising damp may have been a problem (it would have caused adjoining timbers to rot, and spoiled render finishes) but is limited to within about 1.5m of ground level. Condensation (moisture on the internal wall surfaces) would have been more noticeable in masonry buildings. All three sources of dampness would have been insignificant in rooms with well-maintained hypocausts and heated walls.

The timbers at roof valleys would have been vulnerable to decay because these areas would have been difficult to weather effectively (affecting shingles, closeboarding, and any packing to raise the heads of valleys, and more significantly truss timbers, wallplates, and the heads of wall-posts). The mortar here would inevitably crack, allowing moisture penetration, and thus have needed regular repair. (It is fortunate that there were no valleys to barrack buildings, the most numerous buildings.) Oak is not particularly vulnerable to rot, but it could have occurred. Repairing cracked mortar is a relatively simple matter.

Rising dampness might have been significant in timber buildings. Wattle-and-daub would have decayed rapidly unless separated from direct contact with the ground, and low-level cladding would also have decayed relatively rapidly. Rammed-earth or gravel flooring would have needed regular patching or resurfacing. Floor timbers in contact with the ground would have decayed. Roof-coverings might have required extensive repairs after windstorms. Structural damage due to excessive snow-loading could have been avoided by physical removal of snow. The grid-like layout of the buildings within the fortress would have had a funnelling effect on external air-flows, making some areas (mostly around the barracks) very windy. The courtyards would have reduced wind disturbance, as well as affording some degree of quiet and privacy.

The turf-rampart or defensive walls, ditch and counter-scarp bank, and streets would have required considerable and frequent maintenance. It is likely that maintenance teams were regularly employed, particularly for roof repairs, earthworks and streets.

Note I: Phases of the construction of Inchtuthil

Based on Inchtuthil, this summarises the scope of the construction work for a timber-phase fortress.

Phase One: extramural preparation

Camp I: setting-out; site-clearance; ditch-and-bank (excavate; shape and ram); levelling defences. Camp II: setting-out; ditch-and-bank (excavate; shape-and-ram); gateways; surfacing streets; levelling defences. Camp III: setting-out; ditch-and-bank (excavate; shape-and-ram); gateway; adjustments to surfacing; levelling. Outer Masking Earthwork: setting-out; ditch-and-bank (excavate; shape-and-ram); levelling. Western *Vallum*: setting-out; ditch-and-bank (de-turf and set aside; excavate ditch; basket-up, transport and tip; shape; channel; turf). Stores Compound: setting-out; infilling earlier earthwork; site-clearance; ditch-and-bank (excavate; basket-up, transport and tip; shape; gateway; surfacing). Roads: from *porta praetoria* (S) to plateau edge; from *porta decumana* (N) to Tay; from *porta principalis dextra* (W) to quarry; from *porta principalis sinistra* (E) *via* Stores Compound. Temporary Camp at Gourdie Quarry.

Phase Two: officers' temporary camp

Preparation: setting-out; site-clearance; levelling. Timber buildings: Senior Officers' House; shed; Offices I and II; Barracks (two phases). Each sub-divided into: excavate and backfill; structural frame (walls and roof/s); weather-envelope; partitions; openings; and, for Senior Officers' House, stonework. Defences: ditch-and-breastwork to plateau-edge; ditch and rampart; gateways; levelling.

Phase Three: pre-construction

Setting-out defences and main axis: defences and main building-areas; gateways; major roads; minor roads. Site-clearance: large trees; small trees and scrub; ground-cover. Ditch and counter-scarp bank: turfs (cut; lift; transport; place); ditch (excavate; basket-up; transport and tip; shape-and-ram; channel); bank (shape-and-ram; obstruction). Rampart (turf-phase): inner retaining-wall (excavate trench; collect, prepare, and place timbers; backfill-and-ram); rampart (cut and load turfs; transport; unload and place turfs; excavate soil, basket-up and transport; place, shape-and-ram; turf outer-slope); parapet (collect, prepare, place and fix timbers; collect, prepare, place and fix facings); walkway (collect, prepare, place and fix timbers and boarding); access-steps (collect, prepare, place and fix timbers). Gateways: main uprights; tower walkways and lookout platforms; gateway walkway; parapet (framework; cladding); guardrails (rear; lookout platforms); guardrooms (cladding; openings; flooring); gates. Levelling within fortress: streets; building plots.

Phase Four: assemblage of materials

Timber: selecting and felling; primary handling (snedding; de-barking); processing (cleaving and sawing); seasoning?; transporting. Extracted and processed materials: stone; gravel; sand; lime; clay; mortar admixtures; water. Manufactured materials: tiles and bricks; nails; other metalwork; glass?; pigments? Tools and equipment: tools; construction plant; specialist equipment; transport equipment and draught- and pack-animals; horses; personal and military equipment. Food and fodder.

Phase Five: surfacing, drainage and water-supply

Surfacing: streets; accessways; courtyards; open-spaces. Drainage and water-supply: gulleys; channels; culverts; pipework; tanks; latrines; temporary aqueduct?

Phase Six: timber structures

Buildings: Tribunes' Houses; Houses of Centurions of the First Cohort; Centurions' Quarters; Barracks; *Principia*; Hospital; Granaries; *Fabrica*; *Basilica Exercitatoria*; other buildings and store-buildings.

Phase Seven: stonework structures

Built: Defensive wall; ovens; Small Bathhouse. Planned for: Main Bathhouse; *Praetorium*; larger *Principia*. Aqueduct: likely, but unconfirmed.

Phase Eight: abandonment

Demolition of buildings and structures. Removal of materials and equipment. Destruction/concealment of materials and equipment.

3 Site preparation, defences and extramural features

This chapter considers the effort required to prepare the site of a fortress and construct its defences and extramural features. Figure **15** shows a section through Inchtuthil's defences, and **16** shows its extramural features.

Setting-out and site clearance

Setting-out

Fortresses were carefully laid out, with much regularity and symmetry, and efficient use of the defended area. A specialist team probably set out the fortress defences, main axis (gateways and *viae principalis* and *praetoria*), the main building-plots, major streets, defences, and extramural temporary camps. Alternatively, the main outlines of each building could have been set out by a specialist team. Once these main areas were set out, construction work could have begun, in several different areas, by a large number of workmen. Work probably began with the defences, site-clearance and levelling, followed by the main streets and the most urgently needed buildings (barracks and granaries?).

It is not possible to establish exactly how the work was done; options are based on the equipment available, and pragmatism about the building process. Setting-out relies on straight lines, with some apparent adaptation of nominally standard designs to suit local conditions. Equipment need only have been ranging-poles and a means of establishing a right-angle (e.g. a 3:4:5 triangle), with the size of plots gauged by ropes or man-pacing. A level (*chorobates*) could have been used for masonry buildings, but levelling-by-eye and straight-edge would have been adequate for a timber building. One line (say, the central north-south line) could have been marked, with a man-and-pole at each main division point. Off-sets could then be taken from this line, using the same team or additional men. A minimum team of about 10-12 men would have been reasonable, of whom only one need have been experienced.

A cohort-block (six barracks and their centurions' quarters) was approximately square on plan. Whether their arrangement within the fortress determined the overall layout, or vice versa, they were clearly a major factor in the layout of the fortress. Similarly, we do not know whether the size of other building areas was determined by the size of their buildings, or whether buildings were fitted into the space available; some combination of the two is perhaps more likely. Figure **17** shows the approximate widths of the building areas (*scamna*) at Inchtuthil. If the *fabrica*/hospital and tribune's house *scamna* had been the same widths as the cohort-block strips (roughly 20% and 30% larger) the main setting-out would have been simpler, and the fortress only 36m (about 8%) longer. If the widths of

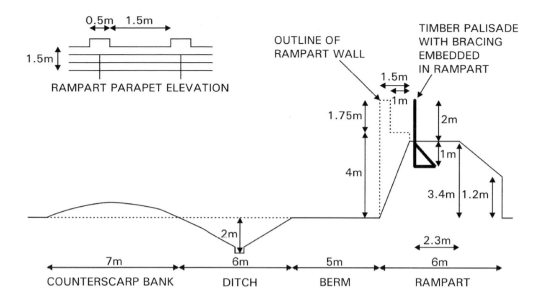

15 *Section through turf-rampart, ditch and bank*

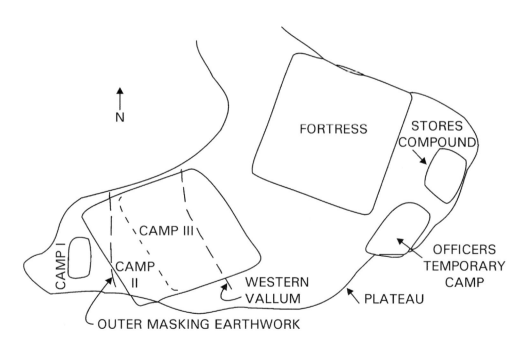

16 *Inchtuthil and its extramural features*

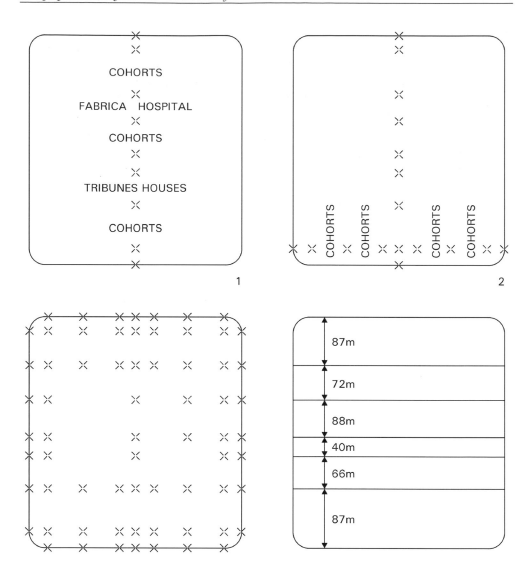

17 Setting-out the main lines of the fortress at Inchtuthil

the *scamna* were in the same ratio as the plan dimensions of these buildings (roughly 1:√2, i.e. 1:1.41) they would have been narrower, at 62m wide. In summary, then, it is not clear why this fortress was laid out as it was, but it was a considered arrangement.

A team of 12 men could have completed the main setting-out in a day (say 100 man-hours). Smaller teams could then have marked the rampart, ditch, counter-scarp bank, and surrounding clear-sight area at closer intervals; completed a detailed setting-out at gateways; and marked the central lines and outer-edges of the streets (160 man-hours). The initial extramural setting out was probably done at the same time (100 man-hours) with later alterations taking a four-man team about 6 hours.

Site clearance

Site clearance, and any necessary levelling, would have preceded the building work. It would not have been necessary to level the whole of a fortress site unless the ground was steeply sloped or very uneven. At Inchtuthil some levelling had been carried out, but it is not clear how extensive this was; the maximum plausible levelling here would have involved removing 51,000m³ of soil.

Site clearance would have included felling trees and shrubs, grubbing up roots and any undergrowth (in situ burning would have destroyed grass needed for turfwork). Forestry manuals, estimators' handbooks and experimental archaeology suggest a felling rate of one man-hour per large tree (450mm or 18in diameter; using a team of two men with axes and two men with ropes to guide the fall) and one man half-an-hour to fell trees of about 350mm or 14in girth. Small trees (up to about 75mm or 3in diameter) could have been felled with bill-hooks or sickles (**18 & 19**), and scrub and undergrowth rough-cleared at 5 minutes per m². These rates are very conservative, and the actual time taken to clear a fortress site would have varied considerably depending on the actual vegetation and climatic conditions.

At Inchtuthil the fortress area (472 x 460m) plus about 20m beyond (say 513 x 500m) must have been cleared completely, an area of about 256,500m². Beyond this, large vegetation was probably removed (say 613 x 600m, a further 111,300m²). In an area of this size there were probably about 400 large trees. A team of four men would thus have felled these in about 400 man-hours, with clearing small trees, scrub and undergrowth taking about 19,200 man-hours, plus removal or destruction.

Excavating, moving and spreading the spoil to level the entire Inchtuthil fortress area (assuming that spoil from one half was deposited on the other half) would have taken about 210,000 man-hours (and considerably more if there was no made-up ground). If levelling were limited to the sites of the principal buildings it would have taken a more plausible 33,700 man-hours. With an allowance for removal of significant localised unevenness to streets and the sites of individual buildings, this suggests a total of about 50,000 man-hours.

Defences and extramural features

Ditch and counter-scarp bank

Inchtuthil's defensive ditch was 2m deep, 6.1m wide with a perimeter of nearly 1,870m. Thus about 11,300m³ of earth had to be dug and removed, using picks, spades and baskets. The height of the 6.7m wide counter-scarp bank is not known; if it were formed of the ditch material it would have been about 1.25m high.

Earth-moving and turf-working, because of the scale of the tasks, were major items; the work-rates were therefore considered carefully. A work-rate for excavating was assessed from analysis of early estimators' books, experimental archaeology and historical records. A Roman soldier was probably less efficient than a Victorian navvy, and a little faster than a Victorian builder, but with slightly less efficient tools: say 1.5m³ per hour for topsoil and 1.25m³ per hour for subsoil. Trenching would have taken longer because

18 Roman sickles. These could have been used to fell small trees and scrub, and cut undergrowth and branches. Museum of London

greater care was needed and the flow of work interrupted, say 0.74m³ per hour (a one metre run of wall-post foundation-trench would have been dug in 21 minutes). The same rate is suggested for backfilling and ramming wall-post trenches. A halving of the rate (i.e. 0.35m³ per hour) for post-holes seems logical, with additional time for very deep holes. These rates exclude basketing-up and removing spoil.

The weight that a workman could lift and carry is a key matter. 50kg is suggested as a reasonable all-day rate for most items, but would have varied with the duration of the task, the length of the working-day, the distance, the size and shape of the item or its container, the weather, and conditions under-foot. A 25kg (55lb) basket-load of earth (plus the weight of the basket) is suggested, to balance weight against speed of the carry, and to allow for awkwardness. A cubic metre of soil was thus equivalent to 72 basket-loads. Baskets were probably transported at the same rate as other man-carried items (1.3 seconds per metre).

The original ground-surface of the ditch (about 10,950m² at Inchtuthil) was probably cut into turfs (about 83,000) to form the base of the counter-scarp bank. At 10 minutes per turf to cut, this would have taken almost 14,000 man-hours. Two-man teams could have moved and positioned each turf in about 1 minute (i.e. 2 man-minutes); a total of almost 2,780 man-hours. The ditch (7,510m³ net of the turfs, and soil for the rampart)

19 Roman hammer and hoes. Originally identified as a hoe, the tool on the left appears to be a carpenter's claw hammer. The remaining tools could equally well have been used to clear scrub and undergrowth. Museum of London

would have taken almost 6,000 man-hours to excavate, produced 540,270 basket-loads of spoil, which (at half-a-minute per load) would have taken 4,500 man-hours to basket-up and 4,500 man-hours to move and tip. Shaping and ramming the ditch sides would have taken almost 1,100 man-hours, and the channel 415 man-hours. A 0.9m high counter-scarp bank would have taken 2,156 man-hours to shape and ram, plus 475 man-hours for an obstruction. The turfwork thus took 16,670 man-hours, the ditch 16,500 man-hours and the bank 2,630 man-hours; a total of 35,800 man-hours. This compares with just over 15,000 man-hours for the extramural earthworks.

Ramparts and gateways

The construction of turf ramparts varied, primarily in the proportion of earth-fill; Inchtuthil's was one-third earth/gravel and two-thirds turf blocks. Turfs had to be cut, loaded, transported, and laid in position, and work-rates are needed for all these steps, some of which would have needed two men. Legionaries were experienced at turf-cutting: the reliefs on Trajan's Column in Rome show legionaries turf-working, and turf-cutter tools were probably standard equipment.

Vegetius describes a standard-sized building turf of 1.5 x 1.0 x 0.5 Roman feet (444 x 296 x 148mm, or approximately 18 x 12 x 6in; 0.01945m^3). This would have weighed about 30kg (66lb), though the weight is largely irrelevant as the load was determined not by weight but by size. The time taken to cut a turf is more difficult to assess. Experimental work (at the Lunt fort), and pre-mechanisation military manuals and estimators' handbooks, all suggest a rate of around 10 minutes per turf. Trajan's Column shows turf carried on a legionary's back, secured with a rope; the Lunt work showed that loading required two men, and that turfs were relatively fragile. Turfs were therefore probably lifted, carried, and placed as one operation. Two men were also likely for unloading and placing (say 5 minutes per turf). Two lifters were thus needed for each turf carried, but could have served more than one carrier. (If the turf-cutter also lifted, his cutting efficiency would have been reduced.) The number of carriers depends on the distance, and the number of lifters on the rate and distance of carrying.

The number of turfs needed was calculated from the volume of a standard-sized turf and the volume of the rampart (assuming two-thirds turf and one-third soil). Inchtuthil's rampart required 18,250m^3 of turf, and 9,125m^3 of soil. This is close to a million turfs (938,355), which could have been cut from an area about 350m^2. The area inside the *via sagularis* was 430 x 418m; the 'surplus' would have been removed, and could have been used in the rampart. (In practice it is unlikely that the entire area would have been suitable for turf-cutting; this approach suggests the theoretical minimum labour requirement.)

The next step is the transporting of the turf. Cotterell and Kamminga (1990) quote nineteenth-century English labourers with 40kg (88lb) burdens travelling 20km (about 12 miles) a day (2.7km or 1.7 miles per hour). This is equivalent to 45m per minute, or one metre every 1.3 seconds. This rate was used as a general rate for all man-carrying on site, to allow for heavier loads (about 50kg, or 110lb) with shorter durations, and also lighter but awkwardly shaped loads. Travel-distances, assuming the most efficient method of moving turfs from where they were cut to where they were incorporated in the rampart, amount to almost 246,000km.

The rampart turfwork involved cutting turfs (156,400 man-hours), loading them onto a man's back (78,200 man-hours), transporting them (38,100 man-hours), and unloading and placing (156,390 man-hours). These times are based on calculating each stage separately. However, the most likely team-size for turf-working was 12 men, which would have been less efficient (there would have been some waiting-time) taking the total to almost 469,180 man-hours. There were further stages too: excavating soil (6,310 man-hours), basketing-up (4,310 man-hours), transporting and tipping (14,785), and shaping, ramming and turfing the front slope (20,655 man-hours). This is a total of about 475,000 man-hours (515,000 if the higher turf-working total is taken).

The simplest construction for the 1.2m high inner retaining wall of the rampart would have been posts (say 100mm or 4in diameter) set earth-fast into the ground (say 500mm, or 20in deep); with a small gap between each post this would have required 16,725 posts (223m^3). The turf-rampart would have had a walkway of timber poles or planks, and a pallisade of planks or hurdles on a framework of poles or posts. (Hurdles would have been quick to erect, with few fixings, would have protected the guards, and have been less vulnerable to wind-damage.) Access steps would have been needed, perhaps 18 or 22 (either side of each gateway; one per cohort block; and perhaps at each corner). A simple construction of 150mm (6in) diameter pole uprights each side, with steps of quartered poles would have required about 5m^3 of timber for each set of steps (**20**).

Excavating the trench for the inner-retaining wall would have taken almost 200 man-hours, but collecting the timbers would take around 7,000 man-hours. If they were cut to length before they were brought to site, and placed against the side of the trench and the adjoining post, then placing and fixing could have been a rapid process (say one man placing and one man back-filling, at 2 minutes per post), taking nearly 1,200 man-hours. The inner retaining-wall would thus have taken almost 8,300 man-hours, and 18 sets of access-steps 12,300 man-hours. The rampart parapet would have taken a total of nearly 5,000 man-hours to build (1,470 man-hours to collect framing and cladding; 925 man-hours to prepare, place and fix the framing; and 2,470 man-hours for the cladding). Hurdles, if used instead of cladding, would have been quicker to fix, but would have had to be made.

The parapet walkway was probably surfaced with planking (say 25mm or 1in thick planks on 50 x 50mm or 2 x 2in joists) or logs (say 100mm or 4in diameter, laid across the width, either whole or split longitudinally). Planking would have required a total of 3,670 man-hours; unsplit logs significantly more labour for collecting (6,255 man-hours), no preparation, and only 800 man-hours to place and fix (7,055 man-hours); and split logs a total of 7,175 man-hours. These options are not strictly comparable as labour for plank and log splitting is excluded. Split logs would been the quickest to construct on site, but planks would have had fewer materials to transport and would have been more stable in use. However, unsplit logs, given a more efficient transport method, might have been the quickest option overall.

Initially fortresses had turf-ramparts, with timber-built gates and pallisades, which were later rebuilt in masonry. Fortresses had four main gateways, presumably of the same design. Figure **21** shows a simply constructed timber gateway, suggested by the post-holes, roadway and rampart details from Inchtuthil's East Gate. Each gateway had two towers, each with nine uprights, 300 x 300mm (12 x 12in), set in 1.5m deep foundation holes, and probably rising 8.5m above ground level. Their lookout platforms were probably not roofed (to prevent excessive wind-loading) and were accessed by fixed ladder. The gates were probably framed and ledged, with two pairs of doors per gateway.

Four gateways would have needed about 135m^3 of timber, of which the main uprights accounted for 60%. Four gateways would have taken at least 11,500 man-hours to construct (5,370 man-hours to collect the timbers, 2,380 for preparation, and 3,760 to place and fix). These figures may underestimate the difficulties of handling the main uprights, particularly if site or weather conditions were not ideal.

Extramural features

Fortresses had features outside the main defences, including temporary camps and work areas, storage areas, a parade ground and roads. These varied from fortress to fortress.

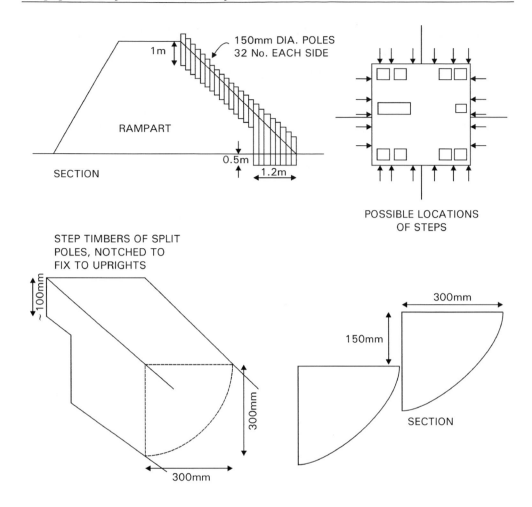

150mm DIA. POLES
32 No. EACH SIDE

1m

RAMPART

0.5m

1.2m

SECTION

POSSIBLE LOCATIONS
OF STEPS

STEP TIMBERS OF SPLIT
POLES, NOTCHED TO
FIX TO UPRIGHTS

~100mm

300mm

300mm

150mm

300mm

SECTION

20 Rampart steps

Inchtuthil, for example, had roads, stores and senior officers' compounds, and three temporary camps with ramparts and ditches, which were later levelled. Camp I's ditch had a volume of about 255m³, and camp II's about 1,860m³ (part of which was levelled when the camp was reduced to form camp III). Camps II and III had timber gateways (requiring about 20m³), and street-surfacing (camp II required about 395m³ of gravel, camp III adjustments about 70m³). These two camps appear to have housed either the construction teams and/or over-wintering troops. There were also two linear features, which may have been atypical: the outer masking earthwork (with a volume of about 210m³) and the 425m long turfed ditch-and-bank named the western *vallum* (with a ditch volume of 2,140m³, and a 6.7m wide bank).

These features would have taken about 40,500 man-hours to construct. The western *vallum* accounted for just over 40% of this, the roads 22%, the stores compound 16%, camp II 13%, camp III 5%, and the outer masking earthwork, camp I and preparation 1%

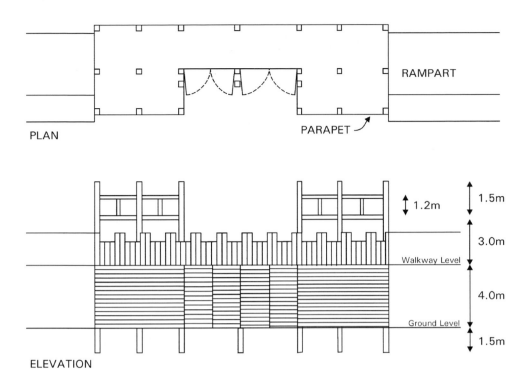

RAMPART

PLAN

PARAPET

1.2m

1.5m

3.0m

Walkway Level

4.0m

Ground Level

1.5m

ELEVATION

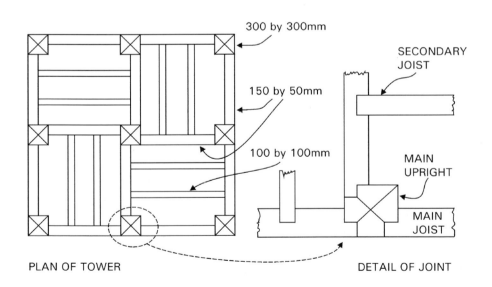

300 by 300mm

SECONDARY
JOIST

150 by 50mm

100 by 100mm

MAIN
UPRIGHT

MAIN
JOIST

PLAN OF TOWER

DETAIL OF JOINT

21 Timber gateways

each. The western *vallum* was thus a significant feature, but may be atypical. Surfacing of roads was also significant, and labour here may have been significantly underestimated. This extramural labour input may seem large, but is equivalent only to, say, 1,000 men working for about five days.

Summary

The pre-construction work to build the fortress at Inchtuthil thus took almost 622,000 man-hours: 260 man-hours for setting-out, 19,600 man-hours for site-clearance (3%), 50,000 man-hours for levelling (8%), 35,800 man-hours for the ditch-and-bank (6%), 505,000 man-hours for the rampart (81%), and 11,500 man-hours for the gateways (2%). The figures for site-clearance and levelling are only tentative, either could have been significantly less, or more. Extramural earthworks (excluding the probably atypical linear earthworks) would have only increased the pre-construction labour total by 3%. The rampart required a major labour input, but only the equivalent of, say, 1,000 men working for 63 days (about 68 days if the ditch-and-bank are included).

4 The timber buildings

This chapter describes the likely design and appearance of the timber buildings of a fortress, and the amount of building material and labour needed for their construction.

Erecting timber buildings

Although there were a variety of different designs of timber buildings, the basic sequence for their construction would have been fairly consistent and is described in **Note II**.

The rate at which the work would have been carried out has been assessed by establishing each step needed to complete each task, and allotting a time to each. Much of this relies on common sense and pragmatism, but can, in general terms, be checked. The four main steps of collect (moving timbers from the main storage area), prepare (joint-cutting, and associated handling), place (moving to position), and fix (securing in position, probably with oak pegs) are considered for each piece of timber, shingle, etc. The work-rates are based on pre-mechanisation estimators' manuals, adjusted to allow for Roman construction, materials and tools. (A detailed explanation of how each rate was established is given in Shirley, 2000.)

The time taken for joint-cutting would have varied depending on a number of factors, some of them apparent (e.g. the size of the timber section; the length of the timber, which would have affected handling; the position of the joint; the type of joint). Other factors, such as variations in the moisture-content of timber, the sharpness of tools, the weather, or the skill and experience of the carpenter, are more difficult to assess. Experienced men, with good tools, and non-extreme circumstances are assumed. If this were not the case, the work would have taken longer.

The main work-rates are summarised in **Note III**.

Construction and design

As no two fortresses had the same layout or complement of buildings it is not possible to give definitive quantities (of materials or labour) for building a typical fortress. This is one reason why Inchtuthil was taken as the main example; it was broadly typical, but other fortresses had variations in the precise positioning, proportions, numbers of buildings they contained, and many contained 'unusual' buildings (e.g. munitions store, bakery, gaol, exercise-hall).

Figures **22** and **23** show how timber buildings might have been framed, and **24** shows how the wallpost-to-wallplate joint might have been cut. The likely construction and

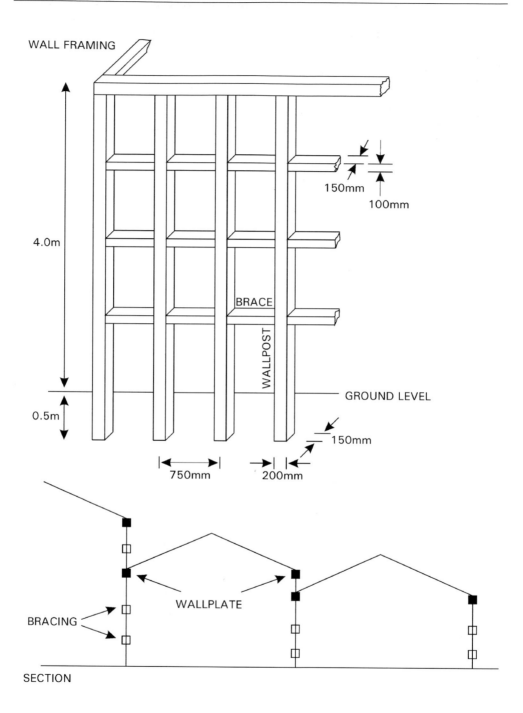

WALL FRAMING

150mm

100mm

4.0m

BRACE

WALLPOST

GROUND LEVEL

0.5m

150mm

750mm

200mm

BRACING

WALLPLATE

SECTION

22 Typical timber wall construction

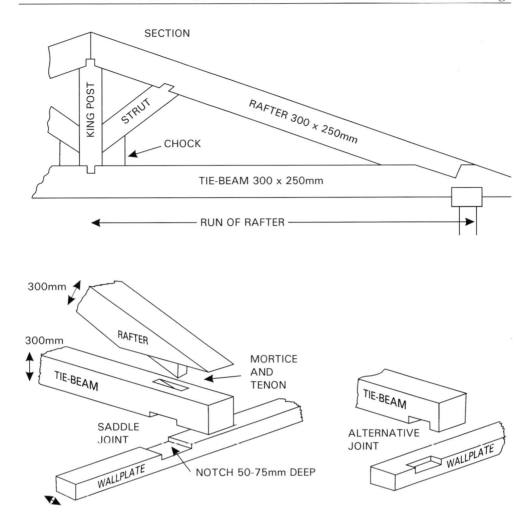

23 Typical roof construction

design of the main buildings in a timber-phase fortress are summarised in **13**, **14**, and **25-35**. These are based on the plans from the Inchtuthil excavation; a detailed discussion of these reconstructions and the resultant calculations of quantities of materials can be found in Shirley, 2000.

Officers' houses and barracks

The four tribune's houses begun at Inchtuthil show a largely unexplained combination of uniformity and dissimilarity. Houses I (**14**), III and IV had four wings around a central courtyard, with two ranges of offices to their eastern end, though house III was 13% larger on plan. House II has an atypical layout, with two courtyards. The reasons for these differences are not clear, but all probably had the same basic construction, perhaps with the status of the senior tribune marked by higher-standard finishes. The five houses of

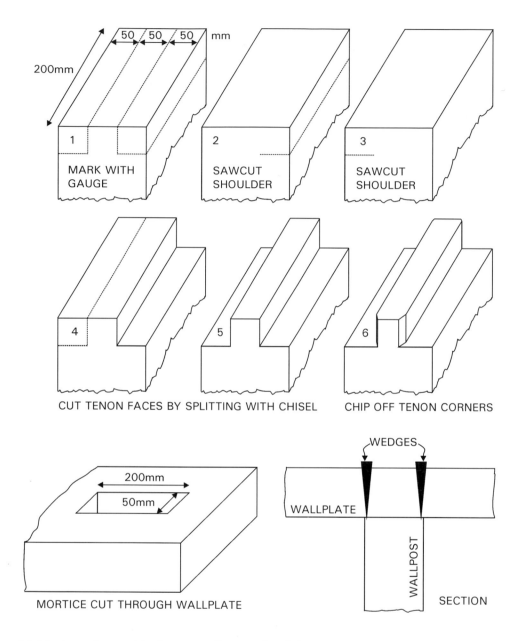

50 / 50 / 50 / mm

200mm

1 MARK WITH GAUGE

2 SAWCUT SHOULDER

3 SAWCUT SHOULDER

4

5

6

CUT TENON FACES BY SPLITTING WITH CHISEL

CHIP OFF TENON CORNERS

200mm

50mm

MORTICE CUT THROUGH WALLPLATE

WEDGES

WALLPLATE

WALLPOST

SECTION

24 Mortice-and-tenon joint between wallposts and wallplates

centurions of the first cohort were similar to but smaller than the tribunes' houses, probably with tiled gabled-roofs, at 20° pitch and 4m main eaves-height.

The remaining 54 centurions' houses at Inchtuthil (**25**) had a simple rectangular ground-plan, about 20-21m long and 11m wide, suggesting a simple gabled-roof. Ridge-heights would have varied slightly as widths vary. They are too wide to have been roofed

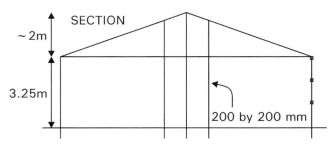

SECTION

~ 2m

3.25m

200 by 200 mm

PARTITION WALLS: 150 by 100mm with
100 by 50mm bracings and 100 by 100mm
headplates.

25 A centurion's house

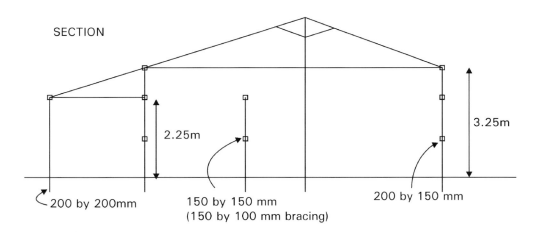

SECTION

2.25m

3.25m

200 by 200mm

150 by 150 mm
(150 by 100 mm bracing)

200 by 150 mm

26 A barrack block

without internal support, and the layout of partition walls suggests a double-line of longitudinal partitions (perhaps either side of a corridor) based on supporting columns. With eaves-height at 3.25m (as the barracks) the ridge-heights would have been similar to those of the senior officers' houses. Roofs may have been tiled or shingled. It is likely that these houses were not simple structures with rough finishes, and they may have had different finishes and fittings.

There were 66 barrack-blocks at Inchtuthil (54 for cohorts II-X, 10 for the first cohort, plus a possible two more, perhaps for cavalrymen). Barracks probably had gabled roofs (**26**), with an eaves-height of 3.25m, though this is not generous for a fully-equipped soldier. Shingled roofs are assumed, as the massive investment of additional timber and

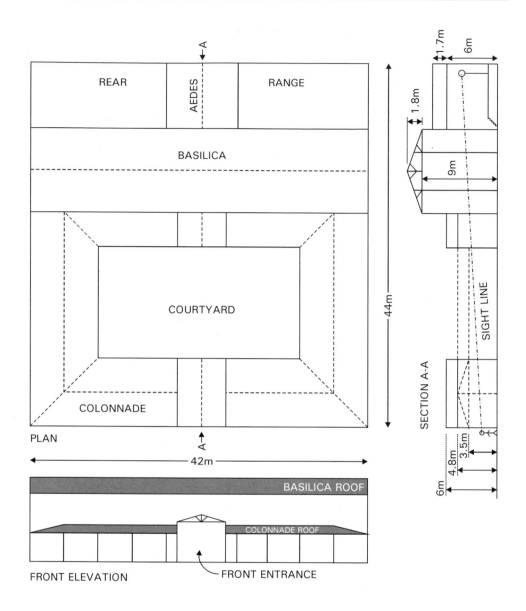

27 A principia *(headquarters) building*

tile seems unlikely in the timber-phase of a fortress. The cross-walls between the *contubernia* are likely to have continued to the roof-undersides (to increase comfort and structural stability) but the longitudinal walls separating sleeping and storage areas may have been lower (say 2.25m). This would have allowed functional separation and increased natural lighting. Floors were probably of rammed earth or gravel.

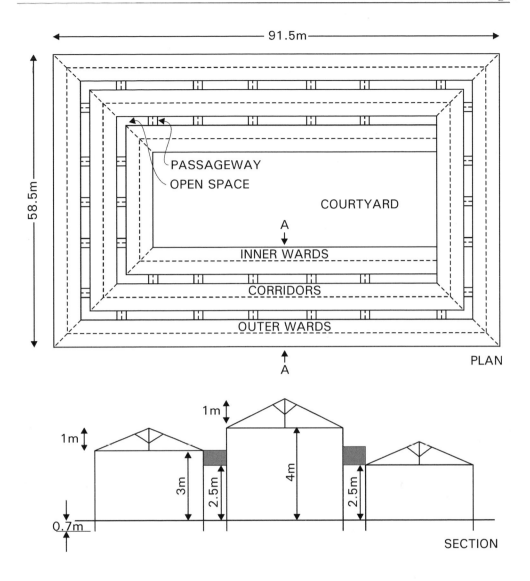

28 The hospital at Inchtuthil

Principal buildings

The *principia* was, perhaps, the most important building in the fortress, and thus likely to have been impressive (**27**). The suggested design has tiled roofs, with the simplest pragmatic arrangement of roof-shapes, with entrances emphasised. Apart from status, there are two main arguments to suggest relatively high eaves: the legion's standards (kept in the *aedes*) were probably visible from the outer entrance, and the post-holes here are much deeper than elsewhere in the fortress. The height of the standard above ground-level (say 4.5m) plus clearance (1.5m) and roof-rise (1.7m) gives an *aedes* ridge-height of about 7.7m. The remainder of the rear-range would have been mono-pitched, say with

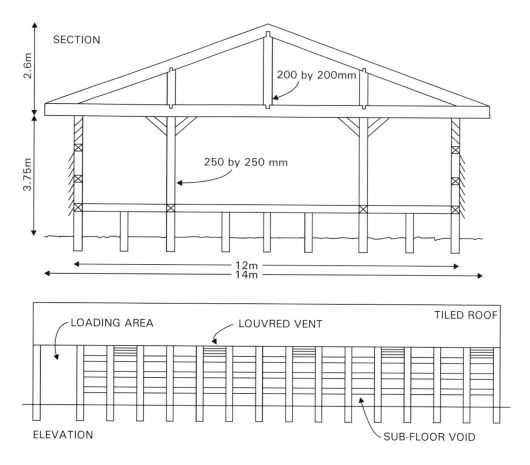

SECTION

2.6m

3.75m

200 by 200mm

250 by 250 mm

12m
14m

LOADING AREA

LOUVRED VENT

TILED ROOF

ELEVATION

SUB-FLOOR VOID

29 Typical section and elevation of a timber granary

the top of the roof at 7.7m and the eaves at 4.5m. The colonnades need only have been about 2m high, but the size and depth of their posts suggests a greater height, about 3.5metres.

The basilica was clearly high, its main posts were 400 x 400mm (16 x 16in), set 1.2m (4ft) deep. Its rear wall eaves must have been higher than 7.7m, say a minimum of 9m to allow for clerestory lighting. The large basilica trusses would have needed secondary posts and struts, and the aisle/nave posts were probably strutted to the trusses. The tie-beam was probably 400 x 300mm (16 x 12in), to allow for the additional timbers, and the eccentricity of mid-span support. Flooring was likely, but its nature is not clear. The excavation found gravelling to the courtyards and inner colonnades only; the *aedes* probably had a raised platform, and perhaps a strong-room below.

The substantial size of Inchtuthil's hospital suggests that it was an important building, probably tiled (**28**). Eaves-heights are far from obvious; a minimum of 2.5m is suggested. Natural lighting of the corridors must have relied on clerestory windows, so the corridor eaves must have been higher than the ward eaves, say a minimum of 4m (trench depths

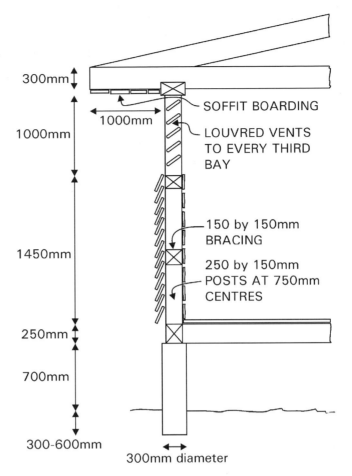

30 Timber granary walling

300mm

1000mm

1000mm

SOFFIT BOARDING

LOUVRED VENTS
TO EVERY THIRD
BAY

1450mm

150 by 150mm
BRACING

250 by 150mm
POSTS AT 750mm
CENTRES

250mm

700mm

300-600mm

300mm diameter

were greater here too). The hospital probably had simple hipped-roofs, and double-pitched passageway roofs. This would have looked better than gabled-roofs, given better weather-exclusion, and have involved very little additional work. There is no excavation evidence for flooring, but there must have been some.

Inchtuthil had six granaries, each about 42 x 12m on plan (**29-32**) and room for two more. Their roofs are likely to have been tiled (to reduce fire-risk and maximise weather-exclusion), with substantial eaves-overhangs. Grain was probably stored in sacks, so door-heights must have allowed ease-of-entry for a man laden with a sack, say a minimum of about 2.75m between floor and eaves. This is also a reasonable height for piles of grain-sacks. The posts probably supported a floor-platform, which must have been high enough to allow good ventilation and maintenance access, say a minimum of 700mm or 28in (950mm or 37in to the underside of the floor). The 14m roof-span suggests intermediate supporting columns, perhaps in pairs, forming a central aisle, and the relatively high roof-rise suggests additional lateral support.

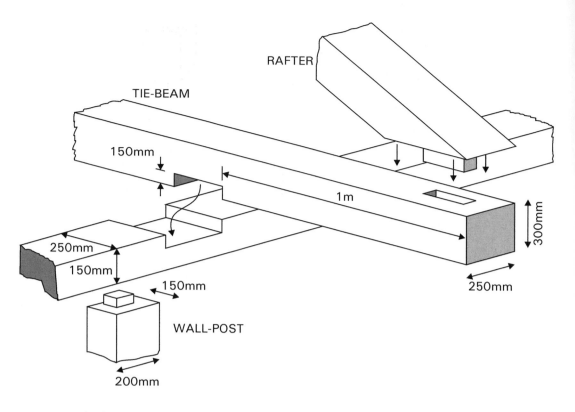

31 Details of roof overhang and jointing for a timber granary

The front-wing of Inchtuthil's *fabrica*, with its wide span and partitions, probably served a different function from the rear-wings, and its plan-shape suggests a slightly different construction (**33**). A gabled-roof is assumed, with a hipped-roof to the rear of the rear-wings (the arrangement of interior posts do not line up for gabled-roofs). The roofs were probably tiled, to reduce fire risk. The rear-wing eaves were probably about 4m high, the front wing eaves about 5m, and the inner walkway eaves 2.5m. The main roofs, with spans of 12.8 and 9.8m, would have needed substantial roof-framing and/or intermediate support.

Other and extramural buildings

Inchtuthil had 176 store-buildings, mostly located along the main streets. These were not simple sheds; their 8m spans suggest substantial structural frameworks (**34**). The timbers were probably of smaller cross-section than for the main buildings, with support taken from columns. Their walkway eaves are unlikely to have been lower than 2m, giving a minimum main eaves height of 2.75m and ridges at about 4.5m, at 20° roof-pitch. Roofs were probably shingled, and the front-walls perhaps open, with removable shutters or doors. The walkway roofs probably did not continue across the gaps between the runs of store-buildings because such canopies would have been vulnerable to wind damage.

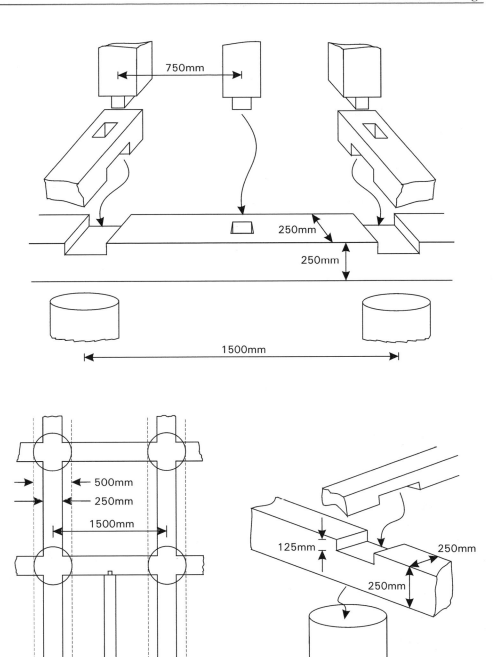

PLAN OF FLOOR GRID

32 Details of timber granary flooring

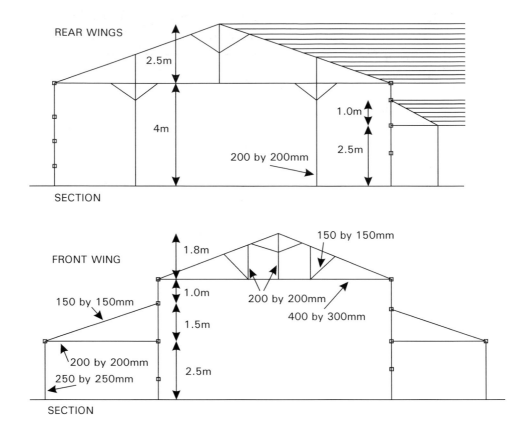

33 The fabrica *at Inchtuthil*

Inchtuthil's *basilica exercitatoria*, although not unusual, may not have been a typical fortress building (**35**). It appears to have been an exercise area, a first cohort 'mess-room', or a specialist workshop or store. The width of the hall, and the necessity for natural lighting, suggest that its walls rose above those of the wings. A gabled-roof is likely for the hall, but the lower roofs were probably mono-pitched (for aesthetics and weather-exclusion), with hipped rear corners. Tiles are likely for reasons of status and/or to reduce fire risk. If the wing eaves were at 2.75m (as the store-buildings), their roof-rise (2.5m) and clerestorey (1m), would give the hall a 6.25m eaves and 8.45m high ridge.

The 11 buildings behind the tribunes' houses were of different sizes and shapes, and probably had different constructions and functions. Two were probably residences (for senior medical officers?) perhaps similar to the tribunes' houses, and there was another relatively imposing building (with a span of nearly 12m, and partitioning). Another may have been a workshop, perhaps associated with the hospital, another an enclosure, and others were probably specialist stores or offices. Roofs were probably gabled, with tiles on the residences (status) and workshop (fire risk) and shingles elsewhere. Eaves-heights

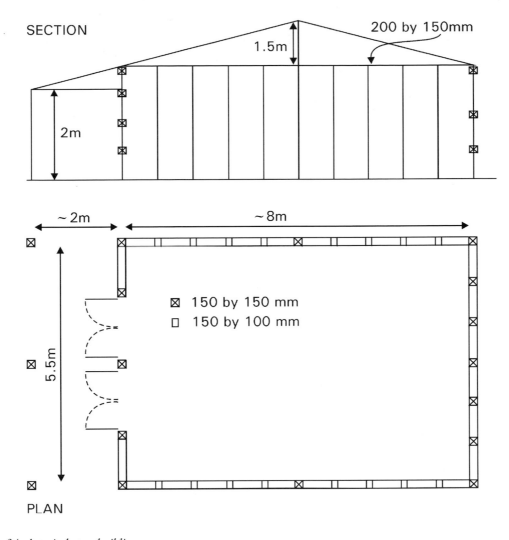

SECTION

200 by 150mm

1.5m

2m

~ 2m

~ 8m

5.5m

⊠ 150 by 150 mm
☐ 150 by 100 mm

PLAN

34 A typical store building

have been assumed at a practical minimum of 2.75m, except where a greater height is suggested by status (residences at 4m) or function.

Timber buildings were also built outside Inchtuthil's main defended area: a substantial residence, three barracks (two phases), a store and two offices. The residence was an unusual and substantial building, both in terms of construction and function, but many fortresses had atypical buildings. It was 10.6m wide, with a hall at least 7.5m high to the ridge, two hypocausted rooms, and a third with a concrete floor (there was also a possible iron-stanchion and a curved run of wall, both unexplained). This was clearly no simple structure; both the residence and the associated small bathhouse seem too grand to have been temporary.

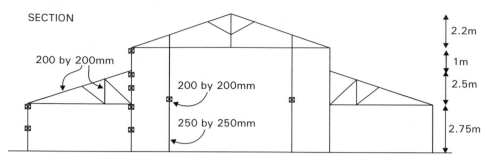

SECTION

200 by 200mm

200 by 200mm

250 by 250mm

2.2m

1m

2.5m

2.75m

HALL WALLS: 200 by 200mm at 750mm centres with
200 by 150mm bracings

35 The basilica exercitatoria *at Inchtuthil*

Quantities of building materials

Materials for the tribunes' houses

A series of calculations (using Inchtuthil's tribune's house I as an example) show how varying the roof-shape, pitch and covering would affect the quantities of materials and labour required. Three roof-shapes were considered: gabled, hipped with equal pitch, and hipped with unequal pitch (each has a different roof-slope area, lengths of ridges, valleys, hips, eaves, and verges, and amount of gable-end walling). Calculations were also made at 20° and 30° roof-pitch for each roof-shape (pitch affects roof-slope area and wall and ridge heights) and for tiles and shingles.

The number of roofing-shingles varied from 15,200 (gabled roof at 20°) to 17,100 (equal-pitched hipped roof at 30°), and the number of *tegulae* from 12,200 (gabled at 20°) to 13,800 (hipped at 30°). The numbers of *imbrices* vary as they are also required at ridges, hips and valleys. The total weight of the roof-timbers and coverings varies from 145-162 tonnes for shingled roofs, and 286-320 tonnes for tiled roofs. At 20° each roof-shape option needed a little over 70m³ of structural-wall timbers, and almost 80m³ at 30°. Once-fixed shingles (at 30°) required 16,950 nails or pegs for a gabled roof, 17,090 for an equal-pitch hipped roof, or 17,030 for an unequal-pitched hipped roof, weighing about 68kg (150lb) if they were nails. This compares with only 2,400 fixings for *tegulae* (weighing about 20kg or 45lb if they were nails). External cladding (at 20° roof-pitch) required around 9,000 fixings (10,000 at 30°), and floor boarding 10,700.

At 20° pitch the largest roof-shape option is 23m² (only 2%) larger than the smallest, and at 30° the difference is less than 1%. The largest roof has 2.5% more *tegulae* (or 2% more shingles) than the smallest (less than 1% at 30° pitch). The difference in the lengths of ridges, valleys, and eaves and verges is, in overall roof terms, very minor. Therefore, in terms of roof-slope area and roof-coverings, the difference between the three roof-shapes is not significant. Roof-shape also has little influence on the amount of timber in a typical roof-truss. The largest shape option required 6% more timber than the smallest (less than

3% at 30° pitch), and when all roof-timbers are considered the significance of roof-shape on quantities of timber is even less significant.

Roof-pitch influences the quantities of roof-coverings and roof-framing, and determines the roof-rise. At 30° the roofs needed 6-9% more main roof-timbers, 10-12% more secondary timbers and roof-coverings, 10-11% more wall-framing, and 13-14% more external cladding, than at 20°. Roof-pitch is therefore a significant influence on the quantities of roof and wall materials.

Tiles weigh nearly twice as much as shingles, and this is clearly of major significance. If shingles at 30° are compared with tiles at 20° (a realistic comparison), the tiles for the gabled-roofs weigh 164% more than shingles. Figures for the hipped roofs are very similar. The roof-covering material has a very significant influence on quantities of roof-framing timber because the heavier tiles need more support. The framing for a 20° tiled roof needs 52-54% more timber than for a 30° shingled roof.

Shingled roofs needed many more fixings (nails or oak-pegs) than tiled roofs because each shingle needed one (or two) fixings, but only one-fifth of *tegulae* had to be fixed. A 30° shingled gabled-roof required almost 600% (14,500) more fixings than a tiled one at 20°. It is worth considering for this reason alone whether, if fixings were nails, a tiled roof might actually have been more 'economic' than a shingled roof. The quantity of roofing-mortar required is relatively insignificant (97m³), but its preparation would have included slaking lime, which is relatively skilled and can take several months. Eaves-overhangs would add a further 3-4% to roof-framing timbers, and 6-7% to roof-coverings and closeboarding. This is significant, but verge-overhangs, at less than 1% extra, are not.

Roof-shape is an insignificant influence on the amount of wall-timbers needed, but roof-pitch is significant (at 30° these roofs required about 13% more than at 20°). The choice of material for enclosing the internal and external walls has a significant effect on the quantities of materials and labour required. External walls required 14-17m³ of external cladding timbers plus 8,700-10,300 fixings, or 61-77m³ of infill. There are practical and performance arguments in favour of, and against, use of timber cladding and wattle-and-daub infill. A main argument against cladding is the high number of fixings (with significant resource implications if they were nails), but speed of on-site installation favours its selection. Timber-flooring, if it existed, would have required a relatively large amount of timber (44m³) and fixings (about 10,700), in itself an argument in favour of solid flooring.

Roof-shape is thus of little significance to the quantities of materials, making less than 3% difference to roof-coverings, and 6% to roof-framing timbers. However, roof-pitch is significant, making about 8-12% difference to quantities of roof timbers, and 10-12% to roof-coverings, and 10-14% to wall-framing and cladding. The choice of roof-covering has a major influence on quantities of roof-timbers, and on roof-covering fixings. For the remaining buildings the simplest plausible roof-shapes have been assumed (usually simple gables), at 20° pitch for roofs likely to have been tiled, and 30° for roofs likely to have been shingled.

With tiled gable-roofs at 20° pitch, the four Tribune's Houses would have needed about 960m³ of main-timbers (1,000 tonnes), and just over 48,000 *tegulae* and 50,000 *imbrices* (415 tonnes). Tiles were therefore very significant. Roof-timbers (trusses, secondary timbers, closeboarding) accounted for almost 65% of these main-timbers (roof-trusses for almost 30%), and wall-timbers (posts, bracings and wall-plates for structural and non-structural walls) for 35%. External-wall cladding would have added a little over 5%, and timber floors almost 20% to the quantity of main-timbers. The main materials are summarised in **Table A**. The weight of these materials gives some indication of the significance of building materials on supply logistics. Other critical factors, largely unknowable, are availability, transport and transportability, and the skill and time inputs (amount and duration) for procuring, making and processing those materials.

Materials for the centurions' houses and barracks

The five houses of centurions of the first cohort at Inchtuthil would have required about 620m³ of main timbers, weighing, with the almost 28,000 *tegulae* and 29,000 *imbrices*, just over 870 tonnes. The roof-timbers accounted for just over half of the main-timbers. External cladding (if used) would have added an extra 8%, internal cladding (if used, to both faces) a further 13%, and timber-flooring (again, if used) about 15% to the volume of main-timbers. The roof-tiles would have weighed about 35-40% of the weight of the main-timbers.

The 54 centurions' houses, if tiled, would have needed about 3,070m³ of main-timbers, weighing 4,380 tonnes with the 139,000 *tegulae* and 141,000 *imbrices*. If shingled at 20°, they would have needed 2,300m³ of main-timbers, weighing 2,815 tonnes with the 173,000 shingles (or 2,450m³ and 3,000 tonnes at 30°). They would also have needed around 220m³ of external cladding. The total weight of roof- and wall-framing timbers and roof-coverings, per building, would have been about 80 tonnes tiled, but only 50 tonnes shingled, for the same pitch. This is significant when considering transporting materials to site.

If the barracks at Inchtuthil had shingled roofs they would have needed 6,800m³ of main-timbers and 606,600 shingles, together weighing 8,500 tonnes, plus 430m³ of external cladding. If tiled, they would have required about 2,300m³ extra main-timbers (about 2,400 tonnes) and roof-coverings would have weighed 3,100 tonnes more. This seems an unlikely investment of resources (assuming that the nearly one million tiles needed could have been produced in time, and transported). Although nominally the same size, the barracks varied slightly, requiring 598-638m³ of main-timbers per six-block cohort (mean 630m³), and 1,160m³ for the first cohort blocks.

Materials for the principal buildings

Inchtuthil's *principia* was untypically small for a fortress, and would probably have been rebuilt in stone had the fortress survived longer. This initial *principia* required 430m³ of main-timbers, 15,900 *tegulae* and 16,300 *imbrices*, weighing nearly 590 tonnes. No *praetorium* (legate's residence) had been built, but a suitably sized and positioned site had been levelled. A *praetorium* would probably have been built in stone as soon as the timber buildings were complete, but if a timber one had been intended initially it would have required a similar quantity of materials and labour to the *principia*.

The hospital would have needed around 860m³ of main timbers (twice that of the *principia*), 42,600 *tegulae* and 44,600 *imbrices*, together weighing about 1,265 tonnes. The hospital had a large amount of roof compared with walls, the roof-timbers accounted for

Table A Summary of materials and labour for the tribunes' houses

	I	II	III	IV	ALL
MATERIALS:					
Roof timbers (m³)	157	133	168	152	610
Wall timbers (m³)	86	96	90	79	350
Total (m³)	240	230	260	230	960
Total (tonnes)	250	240	270	240	1,000
Tegulae (No.)	12,205	11,110	13,095	11,775	48,200
Imbrices (No.)	12,795	11,480	13,735	12,395	50,400
Total tiles (tonnes)	105	96	113	102	416
LABOUR for main-timbers (man-hours):					
Collect	1,150	1,070	1,600	1,840	5,700
Prepare	5,235	3,840	5,530	5,080	19,700
Place, fix	3,600	3,055	3,795	3,495	13,900
Total	10,000	7,965	10,925	10,415	39,300

Figures are based on Inchtuthil and are rounded for clarity (which obscures minor differences between the buildings).

almost 45% of the weight of the main-timbers plus tiles. This is a higher proportion than for the *principia* (37%). The six granaries required 1,330m³ of main-timbers, weighing 1,750 tonnes with the 42,400 *tegulae* and 43,000 *imbrices*, plus 76m³ of external cladding. The floor structure accounted for 32% of main materials by weight, and over 40% by volume, and the granary walls for only 13% of the main-timbers. The *fabrica* needed 520m³ of main-timbers, 33,100 *tegulae* and 33,200 *imbrices*, a total weight of about 810 tonnes. Roof-timbers and tiling accounted for a higher proportion of the main-timbers than for many of the other buildings because of the relatively wide roof-spans. The rear-wings accounted for about 56% of the main-timbers, the front-wing about 28%, and the walkways 16%.

Materials for the other and extramural buildings

The store-buildings (*tabernae*) needed 1,035m³ of main timbers and almost 160,000 shingles, together weighing 1,460 tonnes. They were thus significant in terms of quantities of materials. The *basilica exercitatoria* and its two *tabernae* needed about 230m³ of main timbers, 10,600 *tegulae*, 10,700 *imbrices* and 2,400 shingles, a total weight of about 330 tonnes. Its hall accounted for 40% of main materials, and the two *tabernae* for around 10%. The group of eleven buildings needed 275m³ of main-timbers, 6,600 *tegulae*, 6,800 *imbrices* and 8,400 shingles, a total weight of 360 tonnes. Of these the two residences were the most significant buildings, accounting for almost 20 and 30% of main materials.

The extramural buildings at Inchtuthil required 650m³ of main-timbers (including 220m³ for the residence); about 4% of that required for the fortress buildings. These buildings would also have needed 10,300 *tegulae*, 10,500 *imbrices*, and over 41,000 shingles (about 180 tonnes).

There would probably have been two more granaries and three more tribune's houses if Inchtuthil had been completed. Two more granaries would have needed about 443m³ main-timbers (less than 3% extra to the fortress total), 14,100 *tegulae* and 14,300 *imbrices* (less than 4% extra). Three more tribune's houses would have needed 710m³ main-timbers (increasing the fortress total by just over 4%), 36,000 *tegulae* and 37,800 *imbrices* (increasing the fortress total by a more significant 10%). Together these extra buildings would have increased the main-timbers by 7% (about 1,200 tonnes) and tiling by about 14% (430 tonnes).

Labour requirements

Setting out and excavating

The main setting-out included marking out the main lines of the building plots; within these areas the construction teams must have marked out the lines of the external and structural walls. To some extent they probably relied on rule-of-thumb or nominal sizes and proportions, but there must have been flexibility or the layout of military buildings would show more consistency. This setting-out could have been done by teams of two men (four for the larger buildings), taking nearly 1,100 man-hours for all intramural buildings. Of this about half is for the barracks and centurions' quarters. Wall-trenches would have taken nearly 29,600 man-hours to excavate, and post-holes 2,300 man-hours, a total of nearly 32,000 man-hours. Of this the barracks and centurions' quarters accounted for about 70% of the total.

Structural-frameworks (walls and roofs)

The manhour requirements for the roof- and wall-timbers for the tribunes' houses at Inchtuthil are summarised in **Table A**. Collecting the timbers from the stores would have taken 5,700 man-hours, preparation 19,700 man-hours, and placing and fixing 13,900 man-hours, giving a total of 39,300 man-hours. Structural frames for the three extra tribunes' houses, if built, would have taken a further 43,400 man-hours.

The type of labour (carpenter or labourer) needed for each framing task is also important. Most of the collecting and lifting required labourers, but most of the carpentry work could have been done by teams each comprising a carpenter and labourer/assistant with additional labourers for turning the timbers. The roof tie-beams for house I, for example, needed 9, 10 or 13 labourers (depending on the different roof-spans) to collect, turn and lift the timbers.

Framing the five first cohort centurions' houses would have taken 7,200, 5,300, 5,300, 5,500, and 6,200 man-hours. This total of 29,500 man-hours comprised 5,900 man-hours to collect, 14,900 to prepare, and 8,800 man-hours to place and fix. The structural frame of centurions' quarters XIII needed 1,200 man-hours (collect 200, prepare 600, place and fix 400). The collect times for the other centurions' quarters varied to allow for different travel-distances, giving a total for all 54 centurions' quarters, of almost 72,000 man-hours (collect 18,600, prepare 31,200, place and fix 22,000).

Barrack XVII's frame (typical of cohorts II-X) took 3,200 man-hours (collect 500, prepare 1,600, place and fix 1,100), and the barrack L's (typical first cohort barrack-block) about 4,100 man-hours (collect 1,100, prepare 1,800, place and fix 1,200). The total requirement for all the Inchtuthil barracks is almost 240,000 man-hours (collect 59,000, prepare 108,000, place and fix 73,000).

The *principia*'s wall-framing required nearly 9,000 man-hours, and the roof-framing almost 13,200 man-hours, a total of almost 22,200 man-hours (collect 1,700, prepare 6,300, place and fix 14,300). The basilica roof-framing alone accounted for about 5,000 man-hours. The hospital framing needed 38,200 man-hours (collect 3,000, prepare 23,600, place and fix 11,700), and the six granaries, allowing for the variable collect travel-time, just over 72,700 man-hours (collect 6,300, prepare 35,700, place and fix 30,700). (The two extra granaries, if built, would have taken an additional 45,300 man-hours.) The *fabrica's* framing would have taken a little over 16,600 man-hours (collect 2,200, prepare 7,900 man-hours, place and fix 6,400).

The framing for the *basilica exercitatoria* and its two *tabernae* required a little over 9,500 man-hours (collect 700, prepare 3,500, place and fix 5,300). The eleven buildings behind the tribunes' houses needed a total of almost 9,800 man-hours (collect 1,300, prepare 5,300, place and fix 3,200), of this, the two residences took 3,500 man-hours. The store-buildings required almost 48,900 man-hours (collect 8,900, prepare 24,600, place and fix 15,400).

Weather-envelope, partitions, openings and flooring

Cladding all walls would have taken about 59,600 man-hours, and wattle-and-daub about 68,500 (plus a further 51,100 man-hours for over-rendering). These figures exclude obtaining and preparing the materials, but include mixing mortar and daub. Collecting the materials from the stores is estimated at 22,100 man-hours for cladding, 107,200 man-hours for wattles-and-daub, and 29,200 man-hours for render. Roof closeboarding required about 44,800 man-hours, tiling 40,200 man-hours, and shingling 173,700 man-hours, a total of about 258,800 man-hours (excluding collecting tiles and shingles).

Collecting the partition framing-timbers needed 2,700 man-hours, preparing 7,000 man-hours, and placing and fixing 4,900 man-hours, a total of about 14,600 man-hours. Cladding structural partitions would have required 58,500 man-hours (wattle-and-daub infill about 137,000 man-hours), and non-structural partitions just over 12,000 man-hours (infill nearly 28,000 man-hours). The windows and doors would have taken about 70,000 man-hours (collect 5,800, make 57,500, hang 7,000). Rammed-earth floors would have taken 15,500 man-hours, rammed earth and gravel 87,000 man-hours, or timber 320,000 man-hours.

Extramural buildings

The extramural timber buildings could have been set out and their sites prepared in about 800 man-hours, and built in about 40,000 man-hours (structural frameworks 21,500 man-hours, roof-coverings 13,800 man-hours, wall-cladding 2,800 man-hours, and windows and doors 2,200 man-hours). Many fortresses probably had work camps at some distance from the site; at Inchtuthil, for example, there was probably accommodation at the assumed stone quarry, about 3km (2 miles) away. Two small buildings and a surfaced working and storage area would have taken about 2,500 man-hours, assuming materials were at hand.

Summary of materials and labour for the timber buildings

The main materials required to build a fortress's timber buildings were 16,200m³ of timber for structural roof- and wall-framing; with roofs covered with 366,000 *tegulae* (plus 73,200 nails), 375,000 *imbrices*, 776,000 shingles (plus 776,000 fixings), and 800m³ of mortar. Cladding external walls would have needed 1,100m³ of timber and 706,000 fixings, and internal walls 830-2,600m³, or 17,300m³ of infill. These main-timbers would have weighed, depending on their moisture-content, about 16,720 tonnes, and the roof-coverings about 4,830 tonnes. This is a total weight, for the main materials of 21,600 tonnes. (These figures are based on Inchtuthil, and assume that barracks were shingled at 20° (add 4.6% if at 30°) and that centurions' houses were tiled.)

Of these main materials, 42% would have been needed for the 66 barrack-blocks and 19% for the 54 centurions' houses. Six granaries would have taken 8% of the total, the 176 store-buildings and four tribunes' houses each 6%, the hospital 5%, and the first-cohort centurions' houses, *principia* and other buildings each 3%.

Constructing a fortress's timber buildings would have taken about 1,140,000 man-hours; a considerable labour input, but only the equivalent of about 500 men working for 285 days. However, this figure excludes several other labour-intensive tasks, including the defences, on-site non-constructional labour, and local and non-local preparation and production of food and materials, and transport.

Table B shows how the labour was distributed between the building groups. The barracks accounted for 54% of the effort. **Table C** summarises the total man-hours for each of the main constructional stages. Structural-framing took 52% of the total (598,000 man-hours), and the roof-coverings and wall cladding/infill 30%.

It is also useful to consider how the labour for the structural-frames would have been allocated between the main tasks: for all the timber buildings collecting materials from the stores would have taken 19% of the total constructional effort (600,000 man-hours), preparation 47%, and placing-and-fixing 34%. These proportions vary with the different types of building. Much of the placing-and-fixing work was lifting large timbers (for the *principia* placing-and-fixing took 64% of the effort, because of the massive timbers in the basilica). The significance of variations to on-site transport can be estimated from considering the labour for collecting the materials. These vary from the average 19%, with the *principia*, hospital, and granaries taking about 8%, and the barracks and centurions' houses 25%. Doubling (or halving) these figures, for example, would not make a major difference to the overall total labour requirement for the timber buildings.

Non-structural partitions account for only about 2% of the total labour requirement

Table B Summary of labour for timber buildings, by stage of construction.

STAGE OF CONSTRUCTION	TOTAL MAN-HOURS	PERCENTAGE OF TOTAL MAN-HOURS
Setting out	1,000	<1%
Excavate	32,000	3%
Structural framing	598,000	52%
Weather envelope	340,000	30%
Partitions	85,000	7%
Openings	70,000	6%
Flooring	15,000	1%
Total	1,143,000	100%

Figures are based on Inchtuthil and are rounded for clarity. Structural-framing includes granary floors, and structural-partition framing. Weather-envelope is roof-covering and wall cladding/infill; this figure is for cladding (for wattle-and-daub allow 175,600 man-hours, and over-render 80,250). Flooring is rammed-earth only (allow 86,700 for gravel, or 319,400 for timber). Allow a further 45,300 man-hours for the two 'missing' granaries and 43,400 man-hours for the 'missing' three tribunes' houses.

Table C Summary of labour for timber buildings, by building group.

BUILDING GROUP	TOTAL MAN-HOURS	PERCENTAGE OF TOTAL MAN-HOURS
Barracks	618,000	54%
Centurions'	156,000	13%
Stores	107,000	9%
Granaries	86,000	7%
Hospital	61,000	5%
Tribunes' houses	61,000	5%
1st centurions'	45,000	3%
Principia	29,000	2%
Fabrica	27,000	2%
Small buildings	18,000	1%
Basilica ex.	15,000	1%
Total	1,143,000	100%

Figures are based on calculations for Inchtuthil, and are rounded for clarity. The small buildings are the eleven buildings south of tribunes' houses III and IV.

for the fortress buildings. Many may not have been identified during the excavation, but if the actual number were twice that identified, it would make little overall difference. These figures exclude internal finishes and window-glass, and allow for only basic flooring. It is possible that significant labour inputs might have been involved. These more luxurious aspects of the construction were not essential, and may have been provided (if at all) well after the buildings were functionally complete and occupied.

Note II: Probable sequence for constructing a timber building

This summarises the sequence of work for a 'typical' timber building in a fortress.

Setting-out
The main setting-out of the fortress area included marking the lines of the defences, the main axis, the main building plot areas, and the major streets. Within these main building areas the construction teams themselves probably set out the individual buildings, marking out the positions of the structural walls.

Excavating
This comprised digging trenches and post-holes for the wall-posts, and later backfilling and ramming the earth. It produced a soil surplus (roughly equivalent to the volume of the foundation timbers, plus bulking).

Structural-framework
This is a major element of the construction of the entire fortress, and comprised wall-framing (wall-posts; columns; wallplates; bracings) and roof-framing (roof-truss timbers: tie-beams, rafters, king-posts, struts; secondary timbers; walkway roof-framing). All had to be collected (from the storage area, where some may have been pre-prepared), prepared (cut to length, jointed), placed (moved and lifted to position), and fixed. Some of these operations (e.g. jointing) would have needed only one or two workmen, others (e.g. lifting a tie-beam) would have needed a large team (e.g. 10 or 12). Some operations could have been carried out at the same time, by several teams, of say a carpenter and his assistant, with intermittent help from a larger team of lifters.

Weather-envelope
The distinction between the structural-frame and the weather-envelope (roof-and wall-coverings) is important because until the structural-frame was completed its individual members would not have been stable. The roof-framing would have greatly strengthened the structure, and the buildings could have been left (even over winter) before the weather-envelope was fixed. The framing could have been carried out by one team, or set of teams, and the weather-envelope by others. The weather-envelope work was generally less skilled, and the numbers of men working at any one time more flexible. Alternatively the whole building might have been constructed by the same main team, altering their work and groupings to suit the tasks.

Partitions

Structural partitions are included with the structural-frameworks, but their cladding or infill (which were not structural) are included here. Non-structural walls would have been constructed in a similar way, but with smaller timbers. Positioning of partitioning appears, from the lack of uniformity of layout in officers' buildings, to have often been a matter of personal preference, or to reflect their different roles. Perhaps it also implies that the officers were on site, or full partitioning may have been fitted at a late stage in the construction.

Openings

The rooms must have had doorways, and most probably had doors. Some natural lighting, and ventilation is assumed, and there were probably some glazed windows. Openings are assumed to have fitted between the structural wallposts, probably with wall-bracing acting as lintels. The amount, position and size of openings is very conjectural.

Flooring

This was presumably provided after the main walls, and probably the weather-envelope, were in place, and was not structural (the granaries are an exception). Flooring could have been provided, or upgraded, after initial occupation.

Finishes

Ceilings, plasterwork, painting and mosaics are all possible, but there is no evidence of any at Inchtuthil. If provided they would presumably have been fitted at a late stage, perhaps after occupation, and perhaps at the occupiers instigation and expense.

Note III: Main carpentry and handling work-rates

Each timber joint must be measured, marked out, and cut.

Wall-posts (200 x 150mm, or 8 x 6in)

The wall-posts were earth-fast at their bases, and probably secured to the wallplates with simple mortice-and-tenon joints which would have been quick and easy to cut and assemble. Two men working for 15 minutes each, could have cut the tenon (12 minutes for partition wall-post); two men for five minutes each, could have placed the post and made it earth-fast.

Wallplates (250 x 150mm, or 10 x 6in)

Two men, each 35 minutes, to cut mortice (partition head-plates 15 minutes); two men, each 20 minutes, to cut lap-joint (partitions 10 minutes); one man one minute to cut each wedge; fixing 30 minutes per length.

Bracing timbers (150 x 100mm, or 6 x 4in; 100 x 50mm, or 4 x 2in)

Two men, each three minutes per brace, to cut to length; one man, six minutes per brace, to notch; two men, each 10 minutes per brace, to place and fix.

Tie-beams

Each tie-beam (the heaviest timbers in most buildings) had five joints. The saddle notches are on the underside, and the mortices on the upper face, necessitating turning the timber, allow two men, each one-and-a-half hours per tie-beam; rafter-mortice: two men, each two hours per mortice; post-mortice: two men, each half-an-hour per mortice.

Rafters

The rafter, another heavy timber, had four joints (eight per pair of rafters): the tenon at the rafter foot, a mortice for the strut and for the king-post, and the joint at the ridge. Tenon (this is skilled work): two men, each five hours per tenon, plus extra handling; angle-and-lap: two men, each half-an-hour per rafter, plus extra handling; post-notch two men, each half-an-hour per notch; strut-notch: two men, each half-an-hour per notch.

King-post

Lower tenon: two men, each 20 minutes; upper tenon: two men, each 25 minutes.

Struts

Upper tenon: two men, each 25 minutes; lower cut: two men, each 15 minutes.

Chocks

Two men, each 15 minutes per pair. (It is probable that the tenons would have been cut with a saw, and mortices with chisel and mallet, perhaps with some material removed by drilling. Experimental work by Darrah (1982) showed that mortices can be cut rapidly in green oak with a chisel, and tenons with a chisel and adze.)

Place and fix roof-trusses

Tie-beams: one carpenter and 10 labourers, each one hour; rafters: one carpenter and two teams of six men, each two hours per pair of rafters; posts, struts and chocks: one carpenter and two labourers, each one-and-a-half hours.

Secondary timbers

Housings to purlins: one man, half-an-hour per housing; place and fix: two men, each half-an-hour per 5m length of purlin.

Non-structural partitions

Most rates are the same as for the external-wall timbers, but some rates have been reduced to allow for the smaller cross-section of these timbers.

Windows

The window openings involve minor modification to wall-bracings: half-an-hour per two-man team per piece (i.e. two man-hours); turning dowel ends (e.g. on a pole lathe), one hour for one man per window, plus two hours for one man to assemble the shutters (two per window); placing and fixing, two men each 15 minutes per window.

Doors

Main entrance doors (principal buildings): make 30 hours, hang one hour (two men, each). External: make 10 hours, hang three-quarters-of-an-hour (two men, each). Internal: make eight hours, hang half-an-hour (two men, each).

Carpentry teams

Most carpentry tasks could have been carried out by a team of two men (a carpenter and his assistant). There may have been several teams working on a building (the number of teams is flexible), but it would have been inefficient to have had more than one team working on any one timber. Each team may have carried out all carpentry tasks, though there may have been specialist teams for the more difficult tasks (e.g. rafter tenons), or separate framing and finishing teams.

Handling

Two minutes is allowed to move each timber from each building's site-pile to the place where the joint was cut. The number in the team would vary depending on the size and weight of the timber, but would generally be two men (i.e. four man-minutes). To reduce waiting time this would probably be done by the carpenter and his assistant, but heavier timbers would have needed a larger team. These heavier timbers (e.g. roof tie-beams) would have needed several men to turn them during the joint-cutting.

Closeboarding

Twenty-eight minutes per m² of roof slope area (shingled roofs); 33 minutes per m² (tiled roofs), plus board preparation.

Shingles

Fixing at three-and-a-quarter hours per m² of roof-slope area (roughly 15 minutes per shingle).

Tiling

One-and-one-tenth hour per m² of roof-slope area; 40 minutes (per metre run) for cutting at hips and valleys; 10 minutes (per metre run) for bedding ridges, hips and valleys; five minutes (per metre run) for mortar-finishing at verges and eaves, plus preparation and transport.

Rendering

Fifteen minutes per man per m² of wall area, excludes preparation, but includes mixing (by a labourer), transporting (by a 'hawk-boy'), and applying (by a renderer); a team of three. Adjustments could be made to allow for finer work (i.e. two or three coats).

Wattle-and-daub

Half-an-hour per m³ for installing wattles (plus gathering and preparing), and 15 minutes per m² to apply daub to each face; clay would take about three hours per m³ to puddle.

5 Masonry

Construction in stone or brickwork would have been carried out in two main phases: as part of the initial timber-phase, and the major component of the later rebuilding phase. The masonry component of the timber-phase may, as at Inchtuthil, have been divided into early work (principally the defensive wall) and later work (the *principia*, *praetorium*, bathhouse and aqueduct), which followed on from completion of the timber buildings.

Masonry construction

As timber buildings are relatively simple structures, their superstructures can be suggested with reasonable confidence from limited foundation evidence. But as masonry structures have considerably more plausible options for design, materials and construction, the form of their superstructures must be more speculative. The simplest plausible designs are suggested here as a basis for these necessarily tentative assessments of materials and labour. The main purpose of these estimates is to set the timber buildings and the timber-phase effort into context.

Work-rates for masonry are difficult to establish, except in very general terms, because the nature of the construction, the working method and the labour inputs are somewhat speculative and evidence is limited. Even with a simple structure like Inchtuthil's stone defensive-wall there is limited constructional evidence. Its width is known (about 1.45m) but its height and parapet details have to be assumed. Also, the low-level sections described during the excavation show constructional differences (one section had bonded blocks throughout, most had a rubble core). The work-rates must generalise this variation, and be varied to allow for awkward working.

Rates for other masonry structures are harder to assess. Much of the stonework for ovens at Inchtuthil, for example, is vaulted (built over timber or earth formwork?) which would have been a slow task. Vaulting to buildings would have been much more skilled work, and on a much greater scale. A crude approach is simply to double (or more) the rates; another approach is to spot-price difficult tasks. The calculations for masonry structures are generally less detailed and less reliable than those for timber structures because they are based on design and work-rate evidence which is necessarily more speculative.

Early timber-phase masonry

Defensive wall
The construction of the stone defensive-wall at Inchtuthil varied along its 1,760m run, but the basic assumed design is shown in **36**. Figure **37** shows a detail from Inchtuthil's stone

defensive wall. The foundations required 350m³ of broken stone and cobbles, with 70m³ of mortar for the over-laying bed. The wall itself required 4,300m³ of facing-blocks, 2,600m³ of rubble core, and 3,400m³ of mortar, and the parapets and merlons 860m³ of facing-blocks and 430m³ of mortar. The quantities of facing-stone should be increased by a third to allow for on-site wastage in rough-dressing and laying. Thus the total requirement was for 350m³ of broken stone, 6,850m³ of facing stone, 2,570m³ of rubble, and 3,875m³ of mortar (made from 970m³ lime, 2,900m³ sand, and 580m³ (581,200 litres or 128,000 gallons) of water. At least 1,600m³ of gravel would have been needed for the berm and for infilling between rampart and wall.

The front (angled) portion of the turf rampart had to be cut back, plus a working gap (say 300mm or 1ft wide and 3m high). This spoil must have been removed; if to the counter-scarp bank it would have taken about 14,800 man-hours to excavate and 22,200 man-hours to move. Removing the above-surface timber parapet probably took 1,450 man-hours; thus rampart preparation totalled 38,400 man-hours.

These figures are for constructing the wall, and exclude quarrying and extracting the materials, and transporting them to site. The stone-blocks were probably roughly shaped before being brought to site, with on-site rough-dressing of facing-stones, and mortar-mixing. The foundation trench varied considerably in depth (from about 100-600mm); assuming a 150mm conservative nominal average, it would have taken about 1,200 man-hours to excavate, 250 man-hours to fill baskets with spoil, and at least 2,500 man-hours to move, plus 1,200 man-hours for levelling and preparing. The wall foundation, assuming a similar rate as for masonry, and allowing for awkward working, would have taken about 8,500 man-hours. The wall itself would have taken about 187,000 man-hours, using several teams of masons, each with one or two labourers (the labourers mixing mortar and moving materials). The parapet and merlons would have taken a further 72,400 man-hours, and infilling the gap between rampart and wall

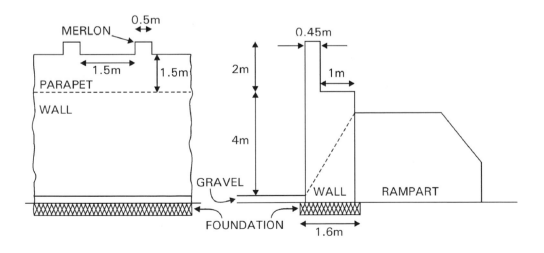

36 Section through the stone defensive wall

37 Inchtuthil's stone defensive wall. This detail shows part of the east wall foundations and fallen stones from the wall. Note their irregular sizes and shapes. Haverfield Bequest

about 13,600 man-hours, with the same labour input for gravelling the berm. This is a total of 340,000 man-hours and is based on very conservative assumptions.

Minor work

Few ovens were excavated at Inchtuthil, but one per barrack (66) was probably intended. If there were also ovens for senior officers, the materials and labour figures should be increased by about 20%. Each oven (with floor, hob, dome-base, and dome) would have had a masonry volume of about 4.4m³; 66 ovens would have needed 193m³ of stone, 24m³ of lime, 72m³ of sand, and 14,450 litres (3,200 gallons) of water. Two men each working half-a-day (eight man-hours) could have selected, cleared and levelled the sites and prepared foundation trenches for the ovens. The construction (at twice the work-rate for the defensive-wall, to allow for the smaller scale of the task and the awkward shape) would have taken 53 man-hours on site per oven, plus mixing the mortar. This is a total of 4,000 man-hours for a fortress's ovens.

The dwarf-walls, concrete floor and hypocaust in the senior officers' house at Inchtuthil, and the hypocaust and associated features in the *primus pilus'* house would have taken about 1,500 man-hours. These may be atypical features in a timber-phase fortress.

Later timber-phase masonry

Principal buildings

The only masonry building built when Inchtuthil was abandoned was the extramural small bathhouse. It had 800mm (32in) thick walls of rough-dressed blocks laid in random courses with a rubble core, on 500mm (20in) deep foundations. Above this, the range of possible constructions is complex. Zienkiewicz (1986) has shown an internal height-to-width ratio for military bathhouses of 1.2:1 to 1.4:1. This suggests 3.5-4.5m *tepidarium* eaves, 6-7m at the top of any vaulted ceiling. The roofs may have been vaulted (either simple barrel-vaulting, running along the short or the long axis, or cross-vaulted), and of masonry or brick, with tiled roofs on a superstructure of timbers. Alternatively, they may have had simple pitched roofs and tiling, in which case the eaves may have been higher, perhaps with internal vaulted ceilings of timberwork and plaster. The roofing arrangements are further complicated by the arrangement of the walls on plan, which preclude a simple roofing arrangement.

Based on a simple construction with 4m eaves, the foundations would have required about 63m³ of masonry and the walls 468m³ (355m³ of stone, and mortar made from 45m³ of lime, 133m³ of sand and 26,550 litres or 5,800 gallons of water). Internal wall finishes (say 25mm or 1in of render and 10mm or ½in of plaster) would have needed 13.5m³ of mortar and 5.5m³ of plaster, plus box-tiles or *tegulae mammatae* to cover 250m² (the internal wall surfaces of *caldarium*, *tepidarium*, and *laconicum*), and paint finishes to 540m². Hypocausts (875mm or 35in high, and assumed to the *laconicum*, *tepidarium* and *caldarium* only, with stone-flags elsewhere) would have required about 670 *sesquipedales*, 2,500 *bessales*, 250 *pedales*, about 300 *bipedales*, and 8m³ of concrete and 3m³ of bedding mortar, plus mosaic to cover nearly 110m². The hot and cold baths would have required almost 9m² of mortar, and the stone-flags 5m³ of flags and 5m³ of mortar. These figures exclude all materials above the assumed 4m eaves-height, and doors, windows and glass, fittings, other decorative finishes, and any treatment of external areas.

The small bathhouse could have been set-out by a four-man team in two days (64 man-hours) and wall trenches excavated in about 1,750 man-hours. The foundations would have taken over 450 man-hours to build, and the walls (from ground-level to eaves, and allowing for curved walling) over 6,000 man-hours. Hypocausts would have taken about 875 man-hours, basic flooring 300 man-hours, and the baths themselves a further 300 man-hours. Basic rendering and plastering would have taken about 800 man-hours, plus fitting boxtiles or *tegulae mammatae*, flues, stoke-holes, etc. Simple timber-framed pitched roofs with tiles would have taken a further 3,000 man-hours. This excludes any additional wall height, and excludes ceilings and decorative finishes.

This estimate of over 13,500 man-hours is very conservative, perhaps unrealistically so, based on a simple structure and local transporting of materials. Adding in the labour to move materials from the stores to site could easily double the labour requirements. (Man-carrying the masonry, flooring and bricks would have taken nearly 22,000 man-hours for a round-trip of 30 minutes, for example.) An overall labour input of 50,000 man-hours for the small bathhouse is thus not unreasonable, plus that for obtaining and preparing the materials.

There is no evidence that construction of the main bathhouse at Inchtuthil had begun, but it would have been planned for, and some materials may have been produced, prepared, and transported. There was a (levelled) site, approximately 75 x 100m, which could have accommodated a bathhouse of, say, 6,000m². (This compares with baths at Chester 6,400m², Caerleon 6,000m², Nuess 5,600m², and Lanbaesis 6,000m².) This would make it about 15 times larger, on plan, than the small bathhouse; it might have been three times higher. An approximate estimate suggests about 25,000m³ of masonry (excluding vaulting) would have been needed for a main bathhouse, plus about 800m³ roofing-timber and about 60,000 *tegulae* and 63,000 *imbrices*. Wall rendering and finishing plaster (excluding ceilings) would have required about 850m³.

Estimating the likely scale of the construction task helps put the construction of the timber buildings in context. Setting-out would have been a highly skilled task, perhaps requiring a specialist team (say 100 man-hours). Excavating foundations and hypocaust voids, backfilling and removing spoil would have taken about 25,000 man-hours; foundation masonry about 7,000 man-hours and wall masonry about 275,000 man-hours; wall-rendering and finishing-plaster about 35,000 man-hours; hypocausts about 15,000 man-hours; other flooring and bath-linings about 10,000 man-hours; and roofing about 50,000 man-hours. This gives a total about 500,000 man-hours including ceilings.

This figure excludes mosaics and wall-painting, and any marble facings or other decorative features; it also excludes fittings, doors and windows (and glass), stoking and flueing arrangements, box-tiles or *tegulae mammatae*, drainage, and treatment of external areas. A total of about 750,000 man-hours to build a bathhouse is suggested to allow for these, but this still excludes off-site preparation and transport of materials. The figures also assume a simple standard of design and workmanship; decorative masonry, roof-vaulting or luxurious finishes, for example, would have required significantly more, and more specialised, labour.

The site for Inchtuthil's *praetorium* (at 65 x 65m it was relatively small in legionary terms) was approximately two-thirds of that for the main bathhouse, and would have required approximately two-thirds of the materials and labour. This suggests a labour input in the region of 500,000 man-hours. The rebuilt *principia* would probably have been as large as the main bathhouse; the prepared site was 70 x 100m. Materials and labour requirements would thus have been of the order required for the baths. The courtyard element would reduce figures, but this would probably have been at least compensated for by a higher standard of finish, and by the demolition of the initial building. Rebuilding the four timber gateways in stone would have taken about 1,000m³ of stone, 100m³ of timber, 3,000 each of *tegulae* and *imbrices*, and about 50,000 man-hours.

Table D summarises the labour needed to build the timber-phase masonry. This shows that the early timber-phase masonry took 365,000 man-hours, and the later timber-phase masonry 2,090,000 man-hours.

Rebuilding in masonry

Rebuilding the timber buildings, in stonework, brick or a combination, would probably have been carried out as part of rolling programme of construction work. How long this would have taken depends largely on the perceived urgency of the work and the resources available, chiefly the numbers of workmen, more of whom would have needed to be more skilled than in the timber-phase. The rebuilding was probably carried out over several years. It is possible to indicate the scale of the task by calculating the necessary man-hours for the on-site construction labour. This was done on the very conservative assumption that the buildings were of simple design.

The barracks would have taken about 1,300,000 man-hours, the eight granaries 400,000 man-hours, the centurions' houses and the store-buildings each 350,000 man-hours, and the seven tribunes' houses and hospital each 250,000 man-hours. The *fabrica*

STRUCTURES	MAN-HOURS
INITIAL MASONRY:	
Defensive-wall	340,000
Ovens (66 no.)	4,000
Small bathhouse	20,000
Officers' houses	1,500
(Total)	(365,000)
LATER MASONRY:	
Main bathhouse	750,000
Praetorium	500,000
New *Principia*	750,000
Gateways	50,000
Drainage channels	20,500
Latrines	4,000
Aqueduct masonry	15,000
(Total)	(2,090,000)
TOTAL	2,455,000

Table D

Labour for masonry in the timber-phase.

Figures exclude hypocausts and boxtiles/tegulae mammatae; doors, windows, and glazing; fittings; and decorative finishes, and obtaining, preparing and transporting materials. Figures are based on Inchtuthil, and are rounded for clarity

would have taken a further 200,000 man-hours, the five first cohort centurions' houses 100,000 man-hours and the *basilica exercitatoria* about 75,000 man-hours, making a total of 3,275,000 man-hours.

This 3.3 million man-hours for rebuilding the timber buildings excludes demolition of the original buildings, labour for windows and doors, hypocausts, flues, stoke-holes and *tegulae mammatae*, all fittings and furniture, and all decoration and treatment of external areas. It assumes a simple design and finishes, and a modest eaves-height. These items and a higher specification could easily have doubled the on-site construction labour. This 3.3 million man-hours also excludes obtaining, preparing and transporting the materials (which is likely to have been more labour intensive than the construction work itself), and all the support labour both on- and off-site, including providing and transporting the food and fodder for the workmen and support staff.

Summary of labour for timber-phase masonry

The masonry built during a fortress's timber-phase would have taken about 2,455,000 man-hours (excluding provision and transport of materials). This labour is summarised in **Table D**. The early masonry work would have taken about 365,000 man-hours (mostly the defensive-wall), and the later masonry 2,090,000 man-hours (mostly the *praetorium*, *principia* and bathhouse). The defensive-wall was thus not a major task. Most of these calculations are necessarily approximate, but do put the construction of the timber buildings (1,143,000 man-hours) into context. Only about 15% of this masonry labour was needed before the timber buildings were completed.

Abandonment or demolition

The fortress at Inchtuthil was abandoned and systematically demolished before all the timber-phase work was completed. Most fortress sites survived long enough to be rebuilt in masonry: this involved demolition of the initial timber buildings.

The abandonment or demolition phase

Demolition for rebuilding is likely to have been a more carefully executed process than demolition for abandonment, and perhaps less urgent. Rebuilding, to reduce disruption, was probably carried out one building at a time or in small groups, but demolition for abandonment was probably a wholesale process. Materials, whether built-in or not, were removed, concealed, or destroyed.

There was some dismantling at Inchtuthil (e.g. gateway main uprights) presumably to allow key materials to be re-used elsewhere, and others were destroyed (e.g. pottery) or concealed (e.g. iron). However, we do not know how extensive or organised any of this was. If the aim was simply to deny the native population the benefit of the materials, then extensive burning of buildings would have been the logical option (with smashing or concealment of materials not destroyed by fire). The majority of the iron found in the hoard at Inchtuthil was in relatively small pieces (i.e. nails). We do not know why it was not removed (iron was a very valuable commodity); perhaps the abandonment process was very hurried, or perhaps transport was limited and only very high-value goods were taken.

We do not know whether the construction work at Inchtuthil was halted and the abandonment process begun immediately, or whether there was first a pause or slowing of the work. This aspect of Inchtuthil's history raises questions about the amount of forward planning (e.g. how far in advance materials were brought to site). The evidence is not conclusive, but does suggest that the abandonment process was careful and thorough, and that the buildings were dismantled. Infilling of drains, for example, suggests that the process was not overly hurried. What happened to these materials though is not clear. If the timbers were burnt, why was the whole fortress not simply fired? If most timbers were removed why was the valuable iron not also removed? Reusing the larger timbers elsewhere seems implausible because of the high costs of transport, the difficulty of working seasoned oak, and the lack of standardisation.

Dismantling buildings and demolishing defences

As we do not know what was destroyed, what was concealed, and what was removed for reuse, it is not possible to calculate the labour required for the dismantling process with much confidence. Only a very general assessment can be made, based on a proportion of the time taken for the construction (excluding collection time, and often preparation time): roof-tiles 100%; structural-frame 50%; roof-shingles, closeboarding, external-cladding, partition-framing and cladding, doors and shutters 25%; and wall-infill 10%. On this basis dismantling a fortress's timber buildings took about 230,000 man-hours, including burning or disposing of the timbers (but not transporting them). This is about 20% of the labour for their construction.

The four Inchtuthil gateways took only 11,500 man-hours to construct; their demolition perhaps took 50% of the time taken for preparing, placing and fixing; about 3,000 man-hours. This might be over generous, but does allow for working around and handling the large main uprights. The stone defensive-wall appears to have been demolished to ground level (remnants of the footings show that it was not completely removed). The demolition perhaps took 25-50% of the construction time, say 70,000 man-hours, but where the stone and mortar debris went is not clear. There was some infilling of the larger drainage-channels, but why this was thought necessary is not clear. Water-storage tanks were perhaps also infilled. An allowance of 10% of the original construction time is suggested, about 2,700 man-hours.

Destruction, concealment and removal

At Inchtuthil, stored pottery was smashed, presumably because it was not practical to remove it. Other domestic items may also have been destroyed, concealed or organised for removal, probably taking 100-500 man-hours. The pit in which the iron nails and tyres were concealed ($30m^3$) would have taken about 100 man-hours to excavate; 500 man-hours is suggested to include gathering, placing and burying the tyres and nails. There may of course have been more than one iron-hoard, and possibly hoards of other materials (a modern examination of the site might reveal more). Although apparently relatively minor, destruction and concealment could have taken significant labour.

Where fortresses were abandoned, removal of materials and equipment is likely to have been a major operation, but is one that cannot be estimated with much confidence because we do not know what was removed, the amount of stores in hand, the equipment likely to have been removed (rather than destroyed or concealed), or the numbers of men on site. It is possible that, because of the high transport costs, no materials were removed, that everything was destroyed or concealed, and only the legion and its normal baggage left the site. If this were so, where are those materials at Inchtuthil? Not all would have decayed in 2,000 years, yet there is no modern evidence for them.

Most construction equipment (e.g. scaffolding, ladders, ropes, baskets) was probably destroyed because of its relatively low value and high bulk, but specialist equipment and some tools were probably removed. This is unlikely to have amounted to more than a few cart-loads (and was perhaps the normal provisioning of a legion). Carts and wagons themselves, and pack-animals presumably went away fully laden. The workforce (legionaries and any non-combatants) presumably marched away, accompanied by the normal allocation of pack-animals and horses (for officers, cavalry, including remounts and any extra provision because of the construction).

6 Streets, drains and water-supply

This chapter discusses the likely nature of the streets and courtyards within a fortress, the foul- and surface-water drainage, and a fortress's water-supply.

Streets and courtyards

Excavation evidence for street surfacing is limited. At Inchtuthil there was some evidence of cambered gravelled streets, side drainage-channels, and significant rutting from carts. Figure **38** summarises the likely minimum layout of surfaced streets at Inchtuthil.

The rammed-gravel surfacing is unlikely to have been thicker than the 200mm (8in) found outside the rear gate; this depth has been assumed for the main streets and the routes to the granaries, 150mm (6in) for the minor streets, accessways and courtyards, and 100mm (4in) between barracks and centurions' quarters. Less than 100mm is unlikely to have been effective. The total amount of gravel required (assuming these depths are averages which allowed for a camber) would have been 3,100m^3 for the main streets, 600m^3 for the minor streets, and 2,800m^3 around the barracks and centurions' quarters, a total of 6,500m^3. The courtyards (tribunes' houses, houses of centurions of the first cohort, the *principia*, *fabrica*, and hospital, and in front of the *basilica exercitatoria*) would have needed a further 820m^3. There was about 84,500m^2 at Inchtuthil not accounted for by the defences, street surfacing (32,000m^2) and buildings (90,100m^2). Some would have been occupied by ovens, latrines, and the like, but if it were all gravelled, to a depth of 100mm (4in), it would have needed more gravel than the street and courtyard areas.

Work-rates for excavating gravel are based on those for earth-moving (1.4m^3 per hour; loading at half-a-minute per basket, and 72 baskets per m^3; and moving baskets at 1.3 seconds per metre). Surfacing probably took about 6m^2 per hour for access areas, 5m^2 per hour for minor roads, and 4m^2 per hour for major roads. These work-rates are based on a pre-mechanisation price-book, adjusted to allow for relatively little ramming (much compacting would have been achieved by the normal use of the roads). These rates are conservative, and surfacing could easily have taken twice as long. The gravel might have come from the fortress interior (perhaps spoil from any levelling) or from gravel-pits outside the fortress. If the work was of a higher standard it would have taken significantly longer.

Surfacing the main streets would have taken just over 8,000 man-hours, the minor streets just over 1,500 man-hours, and the barracks accessways (**39**) almost 8,350 man-hours, a total of almost 18,000 man-hours, plus transporting the 6,500m^3 of gravel (467,600 basket-loads). If the gravel was within 200m, the round-trip to collect, tip and return, would have taken about five minutes per basket, a total collect time of almost

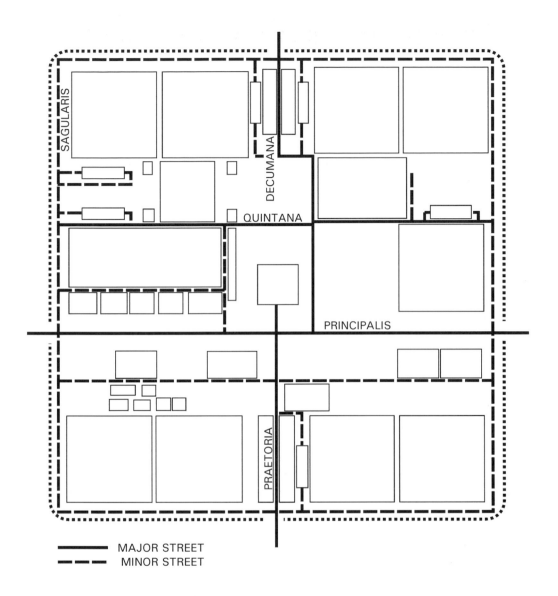

38 Layout of main streets at Inchtuthil

39,000 man-hours. The total labour requirement for a minimum layout of fortress streets would therefore have been almost 57,000 man-hours, plus 7,360 man-hours for the courtyards. If the remaining open-space were surfaced, to a depth of only 50mm (2in), it would have required 2,875m³ of gravel, and taken about 4,200 man-hours, plus transporting the gravel.

Fortresses were probably connected to the existing road network, which would have involved considerable effort. Initially, roads outside a fortress may have been of a very

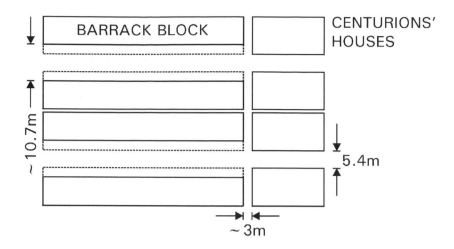

39 Barrack accessways

basic standard, upgraded once fortress construction was completed. Considerable variation is likely, depending on circumstances at each fortress. Approximations were made for the road from Inchtuthil to the quarry. It would have been about 3km long, probably with 150mm depth of gravel and an average width of 4.6m. This gives a surfacing volume of about 1,700m³. Removal of vegetation and other obstructions perhaps took 1,500 man-hours, surfacing at least 2,000 man-hours, and transporting (at only one minute per load) about 1,750 man-hours. This is a total of 5,250 man-hours.

Surfacing within Inchtuthil's extramural camps was a significant task; camp II's streets, (assuming only 75mm or 3in for main streets and 50mm or 2in elsewhere, and a gravel source within 20m of the defences) would have taken about 2,000 man-hours, and later adjustments 1,050 man-hours. The stores compound, if 25% of the enclosed area was surfaced (with 75mm thick gravel from a nearby source), would have taken 2,270 man-hours. Most fortresses would have had a parade ground, though none has yet been found at Inchtuthil. Wherever a parade ground was, it would have needed preparation, clearance of vegetation, levelling and surfacing. No labour calculations have been made for this work as it is too speculative.

Drainage

Foul- and surface-water channels
There is little evidence of the nature and extent of drainage in fortresses, and any assessment can only give an approximate indication of the likely scale and sequence of the work. Drains, either lined or unlined channels or pipe-runs, would have been needed to

take surface-water (i.e. rainfall run-off from roofs and surfaces) and foul-water (e.g. from the bathhouse, hospital and latrines).

Surface-water probably ran to eaves-drip channels or roadside channels, which discharged to larger main-street channels. The eaves-drip channels, connecting channels and minor-street channels were probably not lined initially (so some of their contents would have soaked away into the ground below the channel). The main-street channels would have taken more significant flows, so probably were lined, perhaps initially with timber and later with masonry. Lining would reduce maintenance and ensure that streets were not flooded. Foul-water probably discharged directly to stone-lined channels. Discharge from the fortress was probably via stone-lined channels running through the rampart, and discharged into the ditch or further afield. The Inchtuthil excavation revealed a run of stone-lined channels in the initial timber-phase, suggesting that effective drainage was an important priority.

A simple and somewhat rudimentary initial drainage system is considered here, based on excavation evidence from Inchtuthil and pragmatic assumptions about drainage (**40**). A more sophisticated and comprehensive masonry system would probably have been installed at an early date.

Inchtuthil's stone-built drainage channels were a nominal 700mm (28in) wide and 1,100mm (43in) deep, with 200mm (8in) thick stone-lining and vaulted runs underground. The known channels show considerable size variation, and channel-size would have been varied to take the greater volumes downstream. The minimum likely network is from the hospital and the main bathhouse (both 40m runs vaulted; 110 unvaulted), both running to the rampart-ditch; main road cross-overs (say 80 linear metres vaulted); taking roadside channels under the rampart to the ditch (say 200m vaulted); and from latrines (say 200m vaulted, based on 10 blocks at 20m each). These channels would have required 610m³ of masonry (about 410m³ of stone, and 200m³ of mortar, mixed from 51m³ of lime, 152m³ of sand, and 30,500 litres or 6,700 gallons of water). Excavating these channels would have produced about 1,500m³ of spoil, some of which could have been used for surfacing.

Eaves-drip channels (say 300mm or 12in wide and 150mm or 6in deep) around the buildings may have been roughly level (allowing draining-off only of excess) or have been shallower/deeper at their extremities to allow a fall. Main streets appear to have had timber-lined channels (say 15mm or $\frac{1}{2}$in thick planks), about 750mm (30in) deep and 350mm or 14in wide, and minor streets presumably had smaller channels, say 600 x 300mm (24 x 12in). The timber-lining suggests that they were channels and not soak-aways, and they were presumably laid to falls. This suggests a total channel volume of about 2,800m³, with about 128m³ of timber for lining to the major-street channels and 360m³ of bearers and 135m³ of planking for their covers. Before the aqueduct was built some surface-water (i.e. from roofs) may have been directed to storage-tanks, but the extent of this is unknowable.

The total run-off (rainfall that needed to be drained away) from a whole fortress area can be estimated. Before construction the site would have had a rainfall run-off of about 680 litres per second (0.68m³ per second). Once there were buildings and streets, run-off would have been increased (tiles and gravel absorb less than rough grass etc.), say about

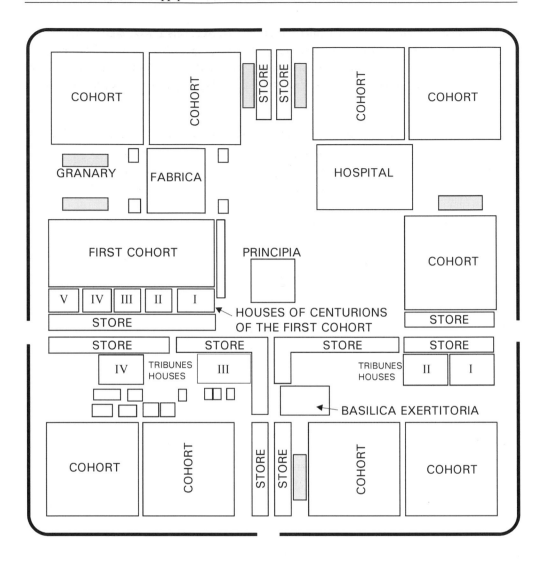

40 Possible drainage/water-supply network

2,270 litres per second (2.27m³ per second). A rough check on the adequacy of these channels is thus possible. The major-street channels would, at 2.27m³ per second rainfall, have held the run-off for a 14 minute heavy rainstorm. This rate and duration would have been unusual, and the delay in water reaching the channels, and the outflow, suggest that flooding or waterlogging would have been rare.

These initial drainage channels would have taken about 6,850 man-hours to excavate, producing about 2,800m³ of gravel or sub-soil (which, if transported, may have been used for street surfacing). Timber-lining (assuming lining to base and sides, and covers at main crossing points) would have taken 6,275 man-hours. The masonry drainage-channels (using increased work-rates to allow for awkward working) to the hospital and main bathhouse would both have taken about 3,340 man-hours, the road crossovers 2,300 man-hours, and the road and latrine runs under the defences each 5,770 man-hours. This is a total of just over 20,500 man-hours. This excludes off-site preparation and transporting materials, which would approximately double the labour requirement, and quarrying or brick production.

Latrines

Masonry latrines and associated drainage-channels are likely to have been built at an early stage, perhaps following on from completion of the timber buildings, but the initial facilities were probably rudimentary. (No latrine-blocks were found at Inchtuthil, but there were small latrines within some principal buildings, though these were probably only timber-lined pits.)

The initial facilities probably comprised a series of soak-aways or pits. A 1911 War Office Manual of Field Engineering indicates the likely provision: five 3ft x 1ft x 1ft trenches, with $2\frac{1}{2}$ ft gaps between, will last 100 men one day; or 15 trenches will last 500 men. Clearly a considerable area of ground would have been needed to allow for this; each day an area about 2.5 x 6.0m would have been needed for every 100 men. Five trenches would have had a volume of 0.4m^3, and would have taken about 15 minutes per trench to dig. Thus one man could dig rudimentary latrines for 500 men in $3\frac{3}{4}$ hours, say 5 man-hours to allow for infilling the trenches from the previous day. Thus every day, 5 man-hours would have been needed per 500 men. If the workforce were, say, 1,000 men for 1,000 days, digging these initial latrines would have required about 10,000 man-hours. This excludes any screening or shelter. This is very tentative; it is likely that more substantial arrangements were built at an early stage.

A simple masonry latrine may have served each cohort (say 5 x 3m with 0.5m wide random-coursed rubble-cored walling, 0.5m foundations and 2.5m eaves, timber-trusses and tile-covering). Each would have required about 25m^3 masonry (17m^3 stone and 8m^3 mortar), 1.2m^3 roofing-timbers, and 170 *tegulae* and 185 *imbrices*. This basic latrine-block would have taken at least 370 man-hours to build (plus providing and transporting materials). This suggests a total of about 3,700 man-hours if there was one block per cohort (there might well have been more, perhaps a block per century). These conservative figures exclude off-site preparation of stone and mortar and manufacture of tiles or bricks, collecting materials from a central stores, and any latrines within principal buildings and officer's houses.

Water-supply

How a fortress's water was collected, stored, and distributed is largely unknown. The initial arrangements would probably have been simple (timber water-barrels on carts?), then a more sophisticated but essentially temporary system pending the completion of an aqueduct. An aqueduct, which could initially have been of earth and timber, would have been a priority as bathhouses required large quantities of water. Labour requirements can only be estimated in the very broadest of terms.

Pipework

There is insufficient evidence to confirm actual pipework networks or the size of the pipes, but conservative assumptions allow the scale of the task to be estimated. Figure **40** shows a possible network of distribution-pipes, from the nominal end of an aqueduct (presumably with a large open/covered tank/fountain/trough) to each of the principal buildings or building-groups, with smaller pipes to some individual buildings. The point of discharge from the aqueduct is not clear, but would probably have been near the bathhouse and hospital (the main consumers; it is perhaps no coincidence that these were usually sited together). A piped supply to each barrack is unlikely during the timber phase. Pipes were probably terracotta (though lead-pipes were found at Chester, and wood and lead at Caerleon and Exeter), 500mm (20in) long with external diameter up to 100mm (4in), laid in unlined channels approximately 150 x 150mm (6 x 6in) in section, running alongside streets and serving the principal buildings only (with barrack *contubernia* drawing water from communal tanks or troughs along the pipe routeways). This notional network suggests that nearly 1,500m of main distribution pipework might have been necessary for a simple system or around 4,000m for a system serving each centurions quarters; it could easily have been much more.

Excavating the pipework trenches (about 30m³) to give the pipes an adequate fall would have taken at least 200 man-hours, and removing this spoil about 390 man-hours. About 2,500 pipes would have been needed; collecting them would have taken about 70 man-hours, and pipe-laying and jointing (at 10 minutes per pipe) 415 man-hours. This gives a total of nearly 1,100 man-hours, but this is a very conservative estimate, and excludes manufacture and transport.

Rainwater

How significant might rainwater have been as a water source? At a conservative estimate of 4.5 litres per day, each man would have required about 1.6m³ a year. The roofs of Inchtuthil's tribune's house I would have received about 870m³ of rainfall a year, but at least 50% must be allowed for evaporation, absorption and leakage, and say 25% for non-collection. Occupancy is not clear but was perhaps around 30 men; they would have needed a minimum of about 50m³ of water a year, a quarter of what might have been collected from rainwater. Water would have been easier to collect from a barrack roof. Inchtuthil's barrack XVIII, for example, would have received nearly 540m³ of water, 25% of which might have been collected (134m³). Eighty men (there may have been more) at 4.5 litres per day, would have needed 131m³ a year. These figures are conveniently close, but the assumptions about losses are somewhat arbitrary. Rainfall run-off could have been a valuable source of water, perhaps a significant supplement to water brought to site, and a valuable tactical reserve. This does not of course allow for water for other purposes.

Water-tanks

A large lead-lined tank and several timber-lined tanks were found at Inchtuthil, and there may also have been others. It is not clear how representative they were, nor is it self-evident that they were for water-storage, or whether part of a piped supply. If they were for rainwater run-off from roofs, it is not clear how it was directed to the tanks, or how silt was dealt with.

A large covered tank found in front of Inchtuthil's *principia* was 1.4m wide, 1.16m deep, and at least 30m long, and probably lead-lined. This may have been for storage of rainwater or for drinking-water brought to site. The roofed area of the *principia* was about 1,400m², with no allowance for evaporation, leakage, or other losses, rainfall to a depth of about 34mm would have been required to fill the tank, a matter of about three weeks normal precipitation. It is not clear how roof run-off would have been directed to this tank. The other tanks, which were probably timber-lined, were of different sizes and shapes, which might reflect a different storage function.

Approximate calculations for materials required for water-storage tanks are based on this evidence from Inchtuthil. This assumes that the tanks were 1.5m deep with a 50 x 50mm (2 x 2in) framework, 15mm ($\frac{1}{2}$in) planking and covers, and that the tank at tribune's house II is typical for tribune's houses, twice the size of tanks of first cohort centurions, and four times those to the centurions' quarters and medical officer's houses, and that the *fabrica* had a tank the same size as the hospital's. On this basis the tank-linings would have required less than 25m³ of timber and only 580m³ would have had to be excavated, but the 115m² of lead-lining to the *principia*'s tank would have been significant. (The fact that only this tank was lead-lined suggests it was important, perhaps for strategic drinking-water storage.)

Barracks might also have had tanks. A tank only say, 3.0 x 3.0 x 1.5m (13.5m³) could have stored a month's reserve (about 11m³). This suggests a total volume of about 1,300m³, which would have taken 7,500 man-hours to excavate, basket-up, and transport (assuming a two minute round-trip). Simple timber-linings of 25mm thick planks would have taken at least 5,900 man-hours.

Aqueduct

Some assessment can be made of the likely amount of water required for a fortress. At a conservative 4.5 litres (1 gallon) for each man and 45 litres (10 gallons) for a horse, 6,000 men and 1,200 animals (one mule per *contubernia*, plus officers' horses and remounts) would have required about 80m³ per day. The bathhouse would have needed a very considerable daily volume of water, perhaps about 300m³, plus any other demands, such as the *fabrica*.

Fortresses may have had temporary aqueducts. At Inchtuthil there is some evidence to suggest a channel or ditch, perhaps with wooden pipes, taking water from the Millhole Burn to the fortress, a distance of about 2 miles (3km). A channel of this size would have taken about 1.3 man-hours per metre-run to excavate and 1.3 man-hours per metre-run to lay the pipes. This suggests a labour input of about 7,800 man-hours, excluding producing and transporting the pipes, setting-out, and building any receiving tanks at the fortress, and it also assumes ease of excavation and access.

Although no evidence of an aqueduct has been found at Inchtuthil it is the logical means of providing water for the fortress, particularly once the bathhouse was built. The existence of pipework fragments shows a sophisticated water-supply system, and this also suggests an aqueducted supply. An aqueduct was a usual means of water-supply to a fortress. An aqueduct channel usually had a depth at least twice its width, and was half-full. A channel 100 x 200mm (4 x 8in) would produce 10 litres per second (2 gallons per second); about twice the volume suggested by the above estimates, but it also allows for losses due to evaporation, and reduced flow due to the relatively high wetted perimeter for this small cross-sectional area. Alternatively, instead of an open channel the water may have flowed within pipework; pipework aqueducts were not uncommon in Roman Britain.

Inchtuthil would have needed an aqueduct about 17.5km (11 miles) long, including 1,000m of (earthen?) embankment with a timber-lining (say 500mm or 20in wide with clay-puddle) or stonework (say 300mm or 12in wide) channel. The embankment would have taken about 140,000 man-hours to excavate, and about 600,000 man-hours to basket-up, move and tip. A further 120,000 man-hours are allowed for shaping and ramming the embankment, and 140,000 for setting-out and repeated checking of the gradient. This is a total of one million man-hours. A stone-lining would have taken only 15,000 man-hours, a timber-lining 5,000 man-hours (both exclude transport and off-site preparation, and any covers). Cutting an open-channel for the remaining 16.5km (10 miles), assuming no significant vegetation or obstacles and easily-worked rock (all optimistic assumptions), with spoil thrown, would have taken a further 500,000 man-hours.

7 Non-constructional work

This chapter discusses the types and amounts of labour required, on site, that were essential for building a fortress, but not directly involved in the construction work itself.

The significance of non-constructional on-site labour

Types of non-constructional labour

The labour calculations summarised and discussed here for a timber-phase fortress are based on Inchtuthil. These types of non-constructional labour would also have been required for the masonry-phase, probably in much the same ratio (relative to the constructional labour) as for the timber-phase.

The 2.4 million man-hours calculated for Inchtuthil's on-site construction work was only a part of the total labour effort to build a fortress. There would also have been on-site non-constructional labour directly or indirectly supporting the construction workers (e.g. cooks, administrators, guards, etc.). There would also have been people working off-site, either locally or at a distance, producing materials, food and equipment, and transporting everything to site. It is not possible to calculate exactly how much non-constructional labour was involved because the evidence is too limited and the range of plausible options too great, but it is possible to identify and discuss the necessary tasks and suggest the likely level of effort involved.

Some personnel may have had more than one role (e.g. labourer one day, cook the next, and weapons training the day after?). Some may have been remote from site, in terms of time as well as location, and may not have been military personnel at all. In one sense the list of people involved is almost endless (e.g. who produced the food which fed the person who bred the pack-mules that were seconded by the army? — the list can be extended to the point of absurdity). This illustrates why a 'total figure' cannot be calculated. It is helpful to identify what effort was specific to the construction of a fortress and what was 'inevitable' anyway. The legion's men, for example, would have had to be fed wherever they were, though their diet and how it was supplied, may have differed, at least during the initial construction period.

The on-site non-construction labour is the men on site who were not directly engaged in the construction work itself. They include those organising and servicing the construction workers, soldiers engaged in military activities (e.g. guarding and training), and sick and injured men. Not all of these men need have been legionaries. In terms of man-hours it makes little difference whether tasks were carried out by soldiers or non-combatants, free-men or slaves, or women, because these activities had to be done. There may have been others on site who contributed nothing to the construction work but required resources themselves, if only food and drink (e.g. senior officers' families, camp followers). The numbers of such people, at least during the construction of the timber-phase, is likely to have been low.

We must also consider off-site non-constructional labour; this may be the major aspect of fortress building. They may have been felling trees locally, or producing iron (in the Weald?), or tiles in a nearby temporary camp. The range of possible locations, and the numbers of men, is vast. Essentially this is the labour required to obtain, by a variety of means, all the food, materials and equipment needed, and get them to site.

Sourcing and supply

The type and quantity of materials, equipment and provisions required had to be determined, and the phasing of that demand estimated. This may have been a relatively sophisticated process, or a very ad hoc approximation based on past experience. Perhaps much depended on the consequences of getting it wrong: delay due to late or inadequate supply, or waste due to oversupply, may not have mattered. Once identified and quantified, the materials and other goods had to be sourced.

Local raw materials were often used by the Roman military, which suggests a thorough reconnaissance of the locality, perhaps by a small team over several days. In overall terms this would have been an insignificant labour requirement, but would have required men with specialist knowledge on site at a very early stage. During the construction phase there is likely to have been further scouting to identify more generally available items, such as fuel, or local game.

Once located, the materials and goods had to be obtained, by requisition, coercion, taxation, or purchase; some could just have been taken (e.g. stone, timber, clay, water). Much of the labour involved in obtaining materials locally would have been for extraction and transport. It is not clear whether imported items (specialist equipment, glass, iron, pottery? etc.) were supplied from centrally held and administered stores, or had to be organised entirely by the fortress planners. Some materials might have been made on site from imported raw materials (e.g. nails from imported iron billets).

Transportation would have been an important stage, particularly where sources were not local. Here the routes, methods and the responsibilities may have been varied and complex. Goods and materials were probably then stockpiled, if only on a short-term basis, to help ensure a constant supply. This would have been important where goods had a lengthy production (or transportation) time, or where demand was erratic but rapid supply vital.

The balance between local and non-local supply is an important distinction, but one where we know very little. Most of the building materials could probably have been obtained locally, or made from local raw materials, but probably not the specialist materials or components (e.g. nails, or iron billets; lead; glass). Common sense suggests that, to reduce transport inputs and offer greater control over supply, timber was obtained locally, and roof-tiles probably manufactured locally. The more luxurious items (e.g. mosaics, samian ware) would have been imported. Basic foodstuffs are likely to have been imported initially, but some local provisioning is likely, if only hunted game, and grazing.

The balance between local and non-local sources could indicate the richness of the local area, in terms of natural resources and native agriculture. It might also indicate what influences the building of a fortress had on the local and regional economy. It could also suggest the organisational abilities, and perhaps the central supply system, of the Roman military. Unfortunately we know so little about their sourcing that it is difficult to go beyond speculation.

Labour for military tasks

Allowance must be made for guarding and protection, military training, unfit and injured men, and those temporarily off-site. Some soldiers probably stood guard (e.g. Vegetius II.xxv) while others constructed the defensive earthworks, perhaps with their weaponry to hand (as shown on Trajan's Column). There may also have been local patrols, and protection of supply lines. The extent of these tasks, and whether they were actually necessary, is unknown. On campaigns the camp tenting arrangements (according to Hyginus) allowed for 16 men out of 80 to be on guard duty. This suggests that at least 25% should be added to on-site construction labour figures to allow for guarding and protection. Building may have been less hazardous once the ramparts were in place, but the reverse could also be argued as the fortress, supply lines and local camps could have become a focus for attack.

Vegetius (II.xii) states that a legionary received weapons training every day, but this may not have happened during the initial stages of building a fortress (itself a form of military training). However, as fortress construction probably lasted more than a year, it is unlikely that no weapons training occurred during this time. It could have been achieved in a variety of ways, for example a set period each day, or a day or more on a rota basis. Some allowance for military training must therefore be allowed, and the equivalent of one hour a day is suggested, increasing the on-site construction figures by about 15%.

It is unlikely that the men were always well and uninjured. Some may have been fit enough to do some work, but with reduced efficiency. Injured men were probably not sent to build, but it is possible that some were injured whilst there, perhaps on protection duties or by the construction work itself. It is also possible that legionary hospitals also served associated forts. The hospital at Inchtuthil was large enough to accommodate 5-10% of the legion, and a high figure is supported by Vindolanda Documents. But unless we assume that a site was under regular attack, a figure of 5% seems ample.

A considerable number of soldiers could be seconded from a legion, or be temporarily away, but this is less likely where a fortress was under construction, particularly if we assume that a full legion had not been sent to build. Nevertheless it is inevitable that some soldiers would have been away some of the time (e.g. carrying messages, acquiring provisions, scouting, etc.). How significant this might have been is highly conjectural, an allowance of 5-10% is suggested.

Labour for on-site organisation

Organisation, administration, and supervision

A construction project of this size would have needed considerable organisation, and at various levels. Labour numbers and skills would have had to be balanced with changing demands throughout the course of the work. We do not know whether the work was organised around the men available, or whether there was sufficient and suitably skilled labour to allow the men to be organised around the tasks. For example, early in the construction a very few specialists would have been needed (i.e. for setting-out) with a high proportion of labourers (i.e. for turf-working, earth-moving, and site-clearance), but as the construction proceeded an increasing number of skilled men (i.e. carpenters, tilers) would have been needed. There is of course no reason why skilled men could not have carried out less-skilled tasks when necessary, but not vice versa. Balancing the labour demands with the labour available, and without loss of efficiency or delaying critical tasks, is a complex matter. We do not know how well it was understood, or what planning methods were used, but some loss of efficiency is inevitable due to organisation being less than ideal.

The work also had to be programmed: to some extent the order in which the various tasks were tackled is likely to have been a matter of common sense, military necessity, and normal procedure. However, it is unlikely that the supply of labour and materials, weather conditions and other influences would have always been ideal. Any 'normal' programme is likely to have been modified, perhaps on a daily basis, to maximise whatever was considered the most critical, or to minimise construction time, or to occupy the most number of men efficiently, or to make best use of any limited or valuable materials.

It would also have been necessary to organise the supply of materials. This was probably the most critical task and the most difficult aspect of the organisation. Some materials would have had a long lead-in time (lime, for example, can take three months or more to prepare), or a long journey (e.g. iron billets from the Weald?), or would simply have been needed in vast quantities (e.g. timber). Unless we envisage a very chaotic and wasteful system, which seems unlikely, the amount of each material needed, and when, would have had to be assessed, at least approximately. With a variety of materials, and a variety of different lead-in times, and changing requirements, this would have been complex.

It would also have been necessary to organise the allocation of the labour-force on a day-to-day basis. How the work was organised is a matter of conjecture. Certainly most of the work must have been done in teams of varying sizes, but whether these were organised centrally, or left to the discretion of, say, each centurion is not known. For example, the workforce may have comprised several centuries, each of which tackled, say, a barrack or a section of the rampart, with the centurion allocating the men and task priorities. Alternatively, the organisation might have been more centralised and uniform and not century/cohort based.

However the work was organised, it took time. How much time, and whether it was a specialised or part-time task, we do not know. Administration would also have been necessary. As the Roman military extensively used written records (e.g. daily rosters, monthly returns) it is highly probable that there was a considerable amount of 'paperwork' associated with the organisation of the construction of a fortress. It seems reasonable to assume organisation on at least two levels, probably undertaken by different personnel: programming the work and ordering the materials, and the day-to-day allocation of specific men to specific tasks.

The workforce would also have needed supervision. This is in addition to any military supervision; the standard of the work and the way it was carried out would have had to be controlled. This was perhaps done by a 'ganger' (the senior member of a small work-team, who worked and supervised/instructed the others). There must also have been higher-level supervision and monitoring of progress, perhaps carried out by some of the organisation personnel.

How much time this organisation, administration, and supervision took is difficult to estimate. To some extent, the more of it there was, the more efficient the actual work was likely to have been. It was all skilled work, some of it highly skilled (if done well). A figure of 5% (of the on-site construction labour) is suggested as a plausible minimum figure; it could easily have been 10% or more. If a ganger-system was used it is likely that more than one man in 20 would have had some (part-time) supervisory role. The 5-10% figure is intended to be an indication of the amount by which the man-hour totals should be increased to allow for these tasks, and not necessarily an indication of the numbers of men responsible.

Stores and preparing materials on-site

Repeated carpentry operations, where there is no need for precision in the length of timbers, could have been carried out away from the building area (e.g. cutting tenons to wall-posts, but not their receiving mortices because these had to be placed precisely). This would have had freed up the construction area, and have allowed more men to work on a building at one time (though some work could have been carried out before the construction work itself began). It would also have allowed repetitive processes to be carried out with more speed. Common sense suggests a carpentry preparation area near either the source of the timbers, or the main storage areas.

It has been suggested that many of the buildings had the same or similar eaves-heights; there is thus a case for on-site or local preparation of 'standard' length wall-posts. The case for standardised roof-trusses is not convincing because the timber-lengths needed are a function of the actual spans of the buildings (which show considerable variation); cutting to approximate length is possible though.

The location of preparatory tasks can influence the collect stage (e.g. timbers cut to length may have required fewer men to carry them), the travel-time of the work-force, lead-in times for materials, and the number of men and possible chaos on site. We cannot determine what happened where, but it is possible to suggest what might have been reasonable. The main materials to consider are timber, stone, and ironwork.

The timber was probably snedded (branches removed) and debarked close to where it was felled, and cut into sections or planks nearby. There were a great many wall-posts of similar length, and these may have been cut to length outside the fortress. This would, theoretically, have taken the same time whether done beside the post-trench, in a preparation area, or at the felling area (though associated labour may have differed). The time taken to measure and cut a post depends partly on its length, but mostly on its sectional-size. The most commonly used wall-posts would have taken 1-3 minutes per cut, plus 2 minutes for measuring and handling, giving work-rates of about 5 minutes, per man, for 200 x 200mm (8 x 8in) wall-posts, 4 minutes for the main 200 x 150mm (8 x 6in) wall-posts, $3\frac{1}{2}$ minutes for 150 x 150mm (6 x 6in) wall-posts, and 3 minutes for partition posts. Teams of two men are assumed (with more men for handling the larger timbers), with one cut per wall-post (assuming felling produces a cut end). These rates are very conservative, and assume efficient processing, good tools in sharp condition, and fit and practised sawyers. The total labour input suggested for this preparatory cutting of main timbers is just over 7,000 man-hours.

Preparation of stone was probably carried out at or near the quarry, this would have avoided transporting waste and would have kept work areas clear. However some on-site cutting, shaping and dressing is inevitable, particularly with the more sophisticated work. Ironworking, largely nail-production, may have taken place on site, or the nails themselves may have been imported ready-made. The size of Inchtuthil's *fabrica* suggests that ironworking would have been a significant on-site activity, though not necessarily during the construction period (and it may also have made nails for other sites). If nails, fittings, tools and other equipment were produced on-site during the construction period, the on-site labour-force would have been larger.

Materials would have arrived at site from a variety of different locations, not all of them local. Much must have been stored before being taken to the sites of individual buildings. The work would have proceeded most efficiently if materials were available before, but not too much before, they were needed. A stores system would have reduced disruption, particularly if some materials were difficult to obtain or transport, had lengthy lead-in times, if planning had not been accurate, or if transport were disrupted. Some goods, particularly those needed in large quantities (e.g. shingles), may have been produced nearby and taken straight to the buildings as needed. Alternatively, such materials may have been produced by a small team much in advance of need, ensuring that materials were ready without large shifts in the composition of the workforce.

A relatively unorganised system of dumping materials as they arrived would have been wasteful of time and materials, and would probably have delayed completion. There may have been a highly organised stores system, with one or more storage areas (some specific to particular materials), with materials collected, recorded, stacked, and ready when needed. The reality is probably somewhere between the two, as there are many factors which could have disrupted even a well organised supply system. However the arrival of materials and their despatch to individual buildings was organised, it would have taken time. How much is difficult to assess, but a figure of 2-5% (of the on-site construction labour) is suggested for staffing the storage areas; associated organisation and administration is included with the general organisation, administration and supervision figure.

Labour for welfare of the workforce, animals and equipment

Welfare is a vague term, partly reflecting our ignorance about the living conditions of the soldiers. We know something of the diet, military equipment and personal effects of a legionary generally, but we do not know exactly what was the norm, particularly for a fortress under construction. We must consider food and drink (its provision and preparation), clothing (provision, and presumably its cleaning and mending), a soldier's personal armour, equipment and weapons (and their repair, replacement, and day-to-day care), and provision and care of personal effects and domestic equipment (cooking utensils, bedding etc.) and any luxury items.

Welfare tasks may have been carried out by legionaries, either full-time or in addition to building work, or by non-combatants. We do not know precisely how many men were in a legion, what proportion of a legion engaged in construction, or how many non-combatants there were. Perhaps this does not matter if our consideration is limited to the total man-hours needed, but it is relevant if we consider the welfare of all personnel. Everyone needed food, clothing and shelter; though the standard of this provision probably varied with status and circumstances.

Some domestic goods would have been part of a legion's normal provision wherever it was, brought to site as part of the normal baggage train. Personal and luxury items were probably limited during the initial construction phase, with increased and upgraded provision once the construction work was well in hand. Finds of samian and glassware at Inchtuthil show that provision (at least of goods in storage) was not basic even at an uncompleted timber-phase fortress. Thus some of the transport would have been bringing domestic and luxury goods.

Provision of food and drink, for the workforce and all others on site, would have taken a considerable time. At first a considerable proportion must have been imported, with granaries and other food-stores probably filled as soon as built. Basic rations were probably supplemented with imported luxury items, and with locally acquired foodstuffs (e.g. from hunting). What was provided, how, and from where is highly conjectural, but whatever the arrangements, they would have involved a considerable labour effort.

Food preparation must also be considered, and collection of water (for drinking, cooking, washing etc.). Food preparation (and perhaps other welfare tasks) was probably organised on a *contubernia* basis (a soldier on a rota basis; a non-combatant?). This might imply that one person in eight, or nine, was needed for basic domestic tasks (perhaps including care of armour and weaponry). If so the on-site construction labour total must be increased by about 14%.

Welfare of animals and care of equipment would have taken two forms, though they may not have been separated: the welfare of animals and equipment normal to the legion, and the welfare of any extra provision during the construction and equipping period. Animals would have needed feeding, grooming, and general veterinary care. There would have been a vast range of equipment (including artillery pieces, and gear associated with horses and pack-animals, and a wide range of specialist tools and equipment), all of which would have needed some level of cleaning and repair. Roth (1991) suggests that the number of men in a legion should be increased by 25% to allow for non-combatants. This is almost equivalent to an extra two men per *contubernia* (perhaps one man was responsible for domestic tasks, and one for looking after the animals and non-domestic equipment). It is suggested here that a conservative 25% should be added to the on-site construction figures to allow for both these types of welfare provision.

Labour for food and fodder, and personal equipment

Efforts to quantify the labour involved in meeting the food and drink requirements, for the on-site construction force and all others on site and nearby, are hampered because we do not know what was supplied, by whom, for how many, in what quantities, where it came from, or how it was transported. The logistics of supplying food, drink and fuel in a frontier zone would have been very different from supplying an established garrison, or an army on the move. Food may have been imported (either officially, or speculatively by merchants, or on the initiative of soldiers), or obtained locally (e.g. by hunting, or official foraging parties). It is unlikely that all basic provisions were available locally, therefore considerable transportation is likely to have been necessary. Allowance must also be made for the provision of associated equipment (e.g. hearths, quern-stones, pots and pans).

Studies of the composition of the Roman soldier's basic diet show a broad agreement: a basic but comprehensive ration, probably supplied by the army but from the soldiers pay, with considerable additional variety. Roth (1991) suggests a basic daily ration to provide sufficient calories and protein for an active man: 850g or 30oz of grain; 40-80g or $1\frac{1}{2}$-3oz of meat; 25g or 1oz of cheese; 50g or 2oz of lentils or beans; 40g or $1\frac{1}{2}$oz of olive-oil; 20g or $\frac{1}{4}$oz of salt; 165g or 6oz of sour wine; this would have weighed about 1.4kg (3lb). Davies (1971) suggests a larger amount of bread, meat, wine and oil, but less variety; it probably weighed about the same. Conservative figures suggest 2.5 litres ($\frac{1}{2}$ gallon) of water daily per man for drinking and cooking (4.5 litres or 1 gallon with basic washing allowance).

Considerable labour would have been involved in producing or obtaining the basic ration, and any luxury items, and transporting them to site. Much was probably purchased or extorted from civilians. How long it took to grow the grain, or breed the animals, is beyond the scope of this book, but it was clearly a significant labour requirement (it also required land, tools and equipment, farm buildings, expertise, etc.). However, it is possible to argue that, as these men would have needed feeding wherever they were, the provision of the food itself (but not its transport) was not itself part of the cost of constructing a fortress.

Transporting food, though, would have been a significant task, not least for the organisers. If we consider just the basic ration (say, 1.4kg or 3lb of food and 2.5 litres or $\frac{1}{2}$ gallon of water per man per day) and assume a workforce of 1,000 men for 600-1,000 days, approximate calculations can be made. These assume basic foodstuffs were imported (by coastal vessel, with pack-mules from the highest shipping point) and that water was moved from the river by four-wheeled cart. For 1,000 men for 600 days, the loading, transporting and unloading of foodstuffs would have taken about 36,000 man-hours (about 58,000 man-hours for 1,000 days), plus about 10,000 man-hours for drinking water (about 16,000 man-hours for 1,000 days). Water would presumably have been moved by the on-site workforce, but some of the food may have been transported by a centrally organised supply team. These figures are just for the transport, and excluding providing and maintaining the transport equipment and the routeways. They also exclude building up a reserve in the granaries.

There is reasonable agreement about the amount of fodder (grain and green-stuff) and water that pack- and draught-animals and horses would have needed, but considerable doubt about the numbers of animals in a full-strength legion or needed during construction. Roth (1991) suggests a full legion had 230 horses (for cavalry and officers, and remounts). If we assume one pack-mule per *contubernia* (there may well have been two) and one large wagon per century, there might have been about 900 mules and 400 oxen for a full legion.

Note IV summarises requirements, assuming half the full-strength numbers of mules and oxen, and 200 horses. This suggests a daily requirement of 3.85 tonnes of grain, 6.30 tonnes of green-fodder, and 19.25 tonnes of water. The grain requirement for animals is about four-and-a-half times greater than that for the men. Green-fodder may only have been provided when pasture was not available, and some may have been available locally (if so, it would have had to be tended, harvested, stored, and animals taken to pasture). Transporting this amount of grain (even if we omit building up a reserve) would have taken a considerable effort. If it were all imported, in the same way as foodstuffs for the men, then transporting grain for 450 mules, 200 oxen and 200 horses, for 600 days, would have taken nearly 110,000 man-hours (175,000 man-hours for 1,000 days). Transporting green-fodder, if all imported, would have taken a further 170,000 man-hours (285,000 for 1,000 days).

Animals were probably taken to the river for water, twice a day, and this would have taken a considerable time (perhaps in addition to the effective working day). It would also have been necessary to surface some of the routeways and the riverside areas. If this watering took an hour a day per animal, and one man could take charge of, say, ten mules or five oxen or horses, this would have taken about 125 man-hours a day (75,000 man-hours for 600 days; 125,000 man-hours for 1,000 days).

Three hundred pack-animals could have moved the fodder and basic foodstuffs in the equivalent of 258 days (assuming 1,000 men, 450 mules, 200 oxen and 200 horses, for 1,000 days). If these pack-animals spent the rest of the year moving local building materials, then half a legion's assumed usual provision of pack- and draught-animals could have coped with the local transport requirements. This does assume that they could operate most of the year, that their use was very carefully planned and organised, and that there were only 1,000 men on site; if these assumptions were exceeded, more animals would have been needed.

Provision of military equipment is unlikely to have been compromised, but parade equipment may not have been present during the initial construction. It is likely that domestic equipment and personal effects were pared down to the minimum during the initial construction period. However, domestic equipment (stone hand-mills, cooking pots and utensils, etc.) was not kept to simple basics at Inchtuthil: finds included samian pottery and glass vessels, though it could have been well below that usual for a garrisoned legion. We do not know what sleeping gear was usual, and there must have been some medical equipment and supplies. Rebuilding is unlikely to have affected provision of non-construction effects, though the amount of domestic and personal effects was probably greater during the construction of the masonry-phase.

What is important here is how the provision of these items was affected by the construction. During the initial construction period, provision of pack-animals, carts and wagons may have been no better, at least initially, than when on campaign. It is likely that additional equipment would have had to be transported, even before the fortress was complete, perhaps as buildings were occupied. Some of this might have been organised directly by the army (e.g. samian pottery), but much might have been organised by the soldiers themselves. Much of the personal military equipment (including some tools) was, presumably, carried by the soldiers themselves when they marched to the new fortress site.

Tools and equipment

It is not possible to estimate the labour needed to provide all tools and equipment used, either directly in the construction or for producing the materials, because the variety and numbers of these tools is not known, and there is no real evidence for work-rates. However, it is possible to suggest what tools and equipment might have been used, and to make some estimate of quantities.

Note V summarises the likely tools and equipment and a selection of Roman carpenter's tools are shown in figures **41**, **42** and **43**. Some of these will have been part of a legionary's or legion's usual provision. Other equipment (e.g. scaffolding), or the amount of it, would have been specific to the construction. The numbers of any tool cannot be realistically estimated, but some outline suggestions can be attempted. Much depends on how many men were working, how the work was phased, and how much was carried out by specialists (who presumably had their own tools). The level of replacement of tools and equipment is also difficult to assess. Iron tools, because of the high labour costs of their provision are likely to have been well cared for, and could be expected to have a long working-life. Less durable equipment (e.g. baskets, ropes, ladders) would have had a short working-life.

Carpentry and masonry were the key building trades, and carpenters and masons probably had their own tools (good work requires good tools, kept clean, sharp and undamaged). The tools would have been of iron (e.g. drill-bits, masonry chisels), iron and wood (e.g. planes), or wood (e.g. mallets), and would have taken a considerable time to manufacture. Work-benches, trestles (and scaffolding) are likely to have been produced on site, probably by the tradesmen themselves. Tools and equipment for tree-felling and preliminary working (e.g. bill-hooks, axes, wedges, ropes) are likely to have been provided on a team basis, with numbers depending on the number of teams. Most of these would have been part of a legion's usual provision, but perhaps not in the numbers required for fortress building.

A roofer (tiler or shingler) is likely to have used a sub-set of the tools used by a carpenter and renderer. The number of tools will have related to the number of roofers actually engaged in this work, but were probably in excess of the legion's usual provision.

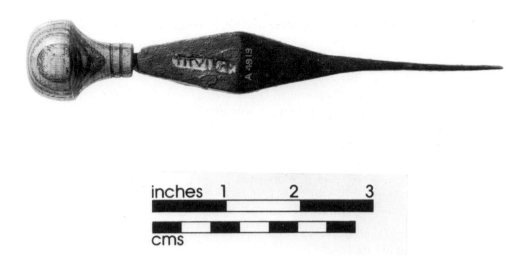

41 Roman awl. A carpenter's awl would have been used to make pilot holes for fixings (e.g. for roof shingles or wall-cladding). Museum of London

Most of the tools for plastering and rendering would have been of wood (e.g. hawks, floats) and thus be under-represented in the archaeological record (no tools were found during the Inchtuthil excavation). Work was probably carried out by a number of small teams (each comprising plasterer, hawk-boy, and mortar-mixer), with tools allocated on this basis. Hawks and floats could have been made easily and quickly on site (say about one hour each, given materials to hand). Some other tools (e.g. spades, shovels, trowels) are likely to have been carried by any garrisoned legion, but additional numbers might have been needed for construction work.

It is not clear to what extent the programming of the work might have been influenced not by critical tasks or numbers of men, or even the supply of materials, but by the tools and equipment available. Large numbers of men could not be engaged in any task unless there were sufficient tools available; it is thus unlikely that vast numbers of men carried out a task over a short period, and more likely that the numbers of men engaged in any task were kept, as far as possible, more or less constant. Double-handling of tools is also possible for some tasks (e.g. two men work, alternately and at a fast-rate, while the other rests). This is the most efficient method if tools are in short supply.

Most men engaged directly in masonry work would have needed a range of chisels and mallets (probably allocated on an individual basis), with lifting gear (ropes, wedges, etc.), and tools for mixing, transporting and laying mortar (probably allocated on a team basis). Each team might have comprised an experienced mason (acting as ganger or overseer), with less-skilled assistants and labourers. The more experienced men probably had a range of specialist measuring tools (plumb-bobs, rules, etc.) and perhaps patterns for formwork (e.g. for arches).

Each trade would have needed labourers (for moving materials, clearing debris, mixing, excavating, etc.). Not all these tasks would have been unskilled, but it is likely that most

42 Roman chisel. A chisel would have been a vital carpenter's tool, used to cut timber joints. Museum of London

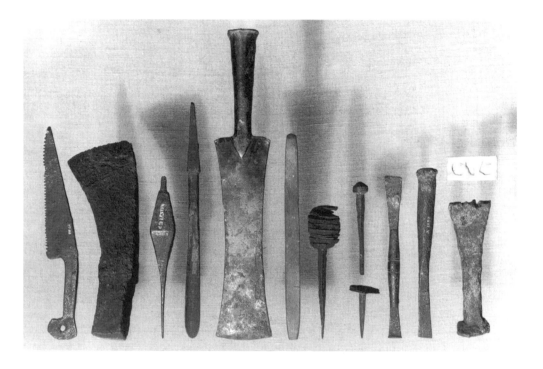

43 Roman carpenter's tools. This selection of carpenter's tools includes a hand-saw, axe head, awl, drill bits, and a whetstone. Museum of London

legionaries could have undertaken most of these tasks, under the direction of more experienced men. Most labourer's tools would have been applicable to most trades, including earthworking (e.g. spades and shovels, ropes, baskets), and although many may have been part of a legionary's usual equipment they are likely to have been required in greater numbers.

Each legion probably had copper-smiths, blacksmiths, plumbers, and trumpet- and horn-makers, but only blacksmiths and plumbers need have been involved in making building materials (the others may not have set up their work-equipment until a fortress was completed). Some of the specialist equipment might have been used in common (e.g. hearths, tongs, hammers, work-benches) and most was probably part of a legion's usual equipment, though quantities of blacksmiths equipment might have been greater if, say, nails were made on site during the timber-phase.

The brick and tile- and lime-burning kilns had to be built, and some tools would have been needed to run them. The number of kilns is not known, but it would probably have been more efficient to have had more than one kiln (at least for bricks and tiles) so that loading and unloading, and firing, could have been organised to even out production and maximise the use of attending staff. The range of tools required by other trades is highly speculative. Window-glass, if cast on site, would have needed furnaces and crucibles, casting troughs, handling and cutting tools, and equipment to handle the raw materials. If decorative finishes were provided (e.g. mosaics, murals), the specialists would have needed their usual range of tools.

Some access-plant would have been necessary. For the lower buildings (e.g. barracks) much of the work could have been carried out from portable trestles, with ladders and pulleys providing roof access for men and materials. Some scaffolding is likely for the higher buildings; it would have been timber (probably small-diameter trunks), secured with rope or leather. Ladders could have been of a similar construction, or similar to a modern timber ladder (more time-consuming to produce, but more resilient and long-lasting in use).

Quantities are difficult to estimate because so little is known about working methods. Provision of, say, two ladders per barrack block might be reasonable, but we do not know how many were being built at once, at a stage that required ladders. It is possible to argue that ladders here were not necessary; men could have climbed up on the scaffolding or trestles, and materials have been hauled up. Alternatively, much of the work, particularly on timber buildings, could have been carried out off ladders rather than providing scaffolding. Timber formwork would have been needed for stonework buildings, to support masonry arches and vaulting, and would probably have been made on site.

Baskets, perhaps made on site, were needed for carrying loose materials. A variety of baskets may have been provided here in addition to the standard issue, and pack-animals may have had basketry panniers. Large numbers of baskets are likely, and would have needed relatively frequent replacement. Water was probably carried in skins or barrels, and slaked-lime in troughs or broken-necked *amphorae*.

Labour to provide timber

Most of the constructional timber probably came from the local area, perhaps with importation of the very large timbers (e.g. gateway uprights) if these could not be sourced locally. Constructional timber was usually oak; the Romans were aware of the different characteristics of different species.

Selecting timbers for felling could have been carried out by a small team, and have overlapped with supervisory, administrative and other organisational tasks associated with the supply of timber. Very large trees (say to produce timbers 300 x 300mm or 12 x 12in and greater) might have taken an hour to select, but smaller trees (200 x 150mm or 8 x 6in timbers) only five minutes. This is a very conservative rate, based on all-day working, and includes associated travelling. The framework of an Inchtuthil barrack block, for example, would have needed about 300 trees, over 80% of 200mm diameter or smaller. A fortress's 66 barrack blocks would thus have involved selecting and felling over 20,000 trees.

Trees of 200mm (8in) diameter could have been felled with axes; say two men, each taking 15 minutes, including clearing undergrowth. On this basis the trees for the frameworks of all the barracks would have taken about 10,000 man-hours to fell. These conservative rates assume ideal felling conditions and do not, for example, allow for felling on sloping ground.

The structural-framework timbers accounted for about 75% of all the timber used in the timber-phase buildings, and the barracks themselves for about 40% of the total volume of timber required for the fortress. Thus the felling man-hours must be increased to about 13,500 to allow for the other timbers, and to 34,000 man-hours to allow for the other buildings, plus 3,500 man-hours for other timbers (e.g. extramurally, gateways, rampart, linings). This is only a rough estimate, and does exclude the extra effort that would have been needed for the few very large trees. Thus felling the constructional timbers would have taken about 37,500 man-hours, and selecting them about 6,500 man-hours.

Before the felled trees could have been converted to timber-sections they would have had to have their branches removed. At a conservative estimate of 20 minutes per tree (two men, each for 10 minutes) this snedding would have taken 35,000 man-hours.

Planks could have been produced either by sawing (using large two-handled saws) or by cleaving (splitting with wedges). Cleaving is more likely; it is quicker, requires less equipment, and produces a stronger plank (cleaving follows the fibres rather than cutting them). Radial splitting is quick and easy, but produces wedge-shaped planks (the tree is split in half, then into quarters, eighths, etc. until the required thickness is reached). These would have been ideal for external cladding, but not for roof closeboarding which requires a flat surface to support the roof-tiles. Tangentially split planks are less wasteful but take longer to cleave, and require more skill as the wedges must be carefully positioned in the end-grain. It also requires timber with a straighter grain than is necessary for radial splitting.

How long this work would have taken is, again, difficult to assess because the evidence is limited. Darrah (in McGrail, 1982) has shown that unseasoned oak can be split easily and quickly using seasoned oak wedges and a beetle (a heavy wooden hammer); a large oak tree can take several hours to split, but a segment from a smaller tree (900mm or 35in diameter and 4m long) can be split in less than two minutes.

A sizeable trunk could have been split into 64 planks: this requires one large split (say two men, each for one hour) and 63 segmental splits (each two minutes to split and two minutes to handle). This is a total of 6.2 man-hours, or 5.8 minutes per plank. Based on a nominal 150 x 4000mm (6 x 160in) plank, about 130,700 planks were needed for external cladding. These would have taken about 12,500 man-hours to cleave (from selected, felled and snedded timber, plus removing debris, stacking and transport). Tangentially split planks for roof-closeboarding would have taken longer than radial splitting, but it is not clear how much longer, say, about 33,500 man-hours, or longer.

Converting the snedded trees into lengths with square or rectangular cross-sections could have been done by sawing, cleaving, trimming with an adze, or hewing. Darrah's experimental work suggests 'a morning' (say four hours) to square a 10m length of 200mm (8in) diameter trunk, using axe or adze. This is probably the quickest method. Cleaving is likely to have taken at least twice as long as adzing (and required more skilled operatives), and sawing much longer.

To estimate the likely scale of the task of converting the timber it is necessary to estimate the number of trees and timber-lengths each one might have produced. As many as 308 trees (701 lengths) would have been needed for a barrack's framework. These figures are increased to allow for the other barracks (multiplied by 66), for the other timbers (plus 25%), and for the other buildings (plus 60%). This gives a rough total of about 70,000 trees (about 155,000 variously sized timber-lengths).

The trunks would have had to be raised off the ground, and turned three times (to allow the face being cut to be in the working position). If a team of two handlers served four adzers (i.e. six men working on four trunks), and each face took 60 minutes to shape and 10 minutes to turn (two men handling, while the adzer rests) it would have taken the adzer 4 x 60 minutes, plus 10 minutes resting-time, say 4.5 man-hours per tree trunk. Turning would have taken two men each 3 x 10 minutes (one man-hour), and the trunk must have been moved to the work-position (say $\frac{1}{2}$ man-hour). The converted timber then had to stacked, to await transport, and debris removed (say $\frac{1}{2}$ man-hour). These times are of course very conjectural, but the significance of modifying any of them can be readily seen. The total time per felled tree was thus about 6.5 man-hours. This gives a rough estimate of about 440,000 man-hours for converting the timber for the fortress buildings (about 485,000 man-hours including the other constructional timbers).

A fortress required about 776,000 shingles (or almost 3,000,000 if all buildings were shingled). If each took a man one minute (to include sawing to suitable lengths, splitting into shingles, and all handling) this would have taken almost 13,000 man-hours (49,700 man-hours for all buildings). Felling and snedding would have taken about 800 man-hours (3,000 man-hours for all buildings). A total allowance of about 15,000 man-hours, including preparation of the working area is suggested (about 55,000 man-hours if all buildings were shingled); this is very conservative.

An estimate of the time for producing wattles can also be made. The fortress buildings had a total wall surface-area of about 115,333m² (92,000m² net of the wall-timbers themselves). Wattling is likely to have comprised hazel or birch stakes, say about 10-15mm diameter, let into holes drilled in the timbers, with hazel twigs woven around them to support the daub. With wall-posts at 750mm centres, six stakes per space seems reasonable; about seven linear-metres of stakes per square-metre of net wall-area. This is a total of about 66,000 linear-metres (each stake would have been, on average, a little less than a metre long). These would have had to be cut (roughly to the correct length) and snedded. If each took only two minutes, this would have taken roughly 2,200 man-hours, excluding preparing their ends. Cutting the hazel twigs could hardly have taken less time, giving a very conservative total of about 4,500 man-hours for cutting the wattles, twice that if wattle-and-daub were applied to both faces.

Labour to extract and process materials

The main materials requiring extraction and processing were stone, gravel and sand, lime, daub, water (for building), and fuel (for processing).

Stone was probably roughly dressed at the quarry, to reduce transport of waste. The rates given in Victorian estimators' handbooks suggest that it would have taken about 3.6 man-hours/m^3 to quarry stone of the type used at Inchtuthil. For Roman working this is a very conservative rate, which assumes easily worked sedimentary rock, split with wedges along natural fissures and bedding planes, from accessible surface deposits. In non-ideal conditions quarrying would have taken very significantly longer, as suggested by Anderson's rate (1992) of over 3 man-days/m^3.

The volume of stone required must be increased by about one-third to allow for dressing and shaping on site, plus wastage at the quarry, say a total of about 50%. Thus quarrying stone for the timber-phase (including the defensive wall) would have taken at least 56,000 man-hours, or nearer 560,000 man-hours if we take the higher rate. This is very significant. These figures, like all others for extracting and processing materials, exclude setting up the work-area and its equipment, organisation and administration, the welfare of the workforce, and transport.

About 7,300m^3 of gravel was used for fortress surfacing, and about 1,600m^3 for the berm around the wall. Effort for excavating this gravel has been included in the main labour figures, but not the time taken to locate it, remove any earth-cover, or perform any possible sieving and grading, or washing. This work is so speculative that even an approximation cannot reasonably be made. The sand required would have taken about 4,800 man-hours to excavate, longer if it were deeper than shovel-depth.

The mortar would probably have been about 25% lime (by volume of dry ingredients), but would have been used in the form of slaked-lime (wet, and about 60% bulkier). At Inchtuthil the stonework-mortar needed 1,000m^3, roofing-mortar 200m^3 and over-rendering of external walls 430m^3, plus any for internal plastering or concreting.

Lime production was a relatively skilled and hazardous task, and took a considerable time. Dix (1982) suggests three weeks to burn, and at least two weeks to slake, and usually three months to mature. Estimates of labour for these tasks can only be very approximate. Quarrying is likely to have taken about 6,000 man-hours (or 10 times longer if the higher work-rate is used). Crushing and preparing for burning perhaps took as long again (6,000 man-hours), lime-burning about 150,000 man-hours, and slaking at least a further 12,000, a total of about 175,000 man-hours. This excludes operating the quarry, building the kilns, transport, providing and crushing the admixture, and providing water and fuel.

The external walls of the timber-phase buildings would have needed about 3,850m^3 of daub (allowing for structural timbers, wattles, voids and cavities). This would have been clay, made workable by puddling, and less vulnerable to cracking by an admixture (e.g. animal hair, straw). This would have taken about 3,100 man-hours to excavate (longer if thrown or hauled). An overall allowance of about 10,000 man-hours is suggested for the provision of daub, including weathering and puddling, but excluding admixtures and transport.

Water would have been needed for mixing mortar and daub, slaking lime, producing tiles, and for iron-working, and soaking tiles and bricks (in dry weather) prior to mortaring. Timber-phase buildings would have needed about 4,800m^3 of mortar and 3,850m^3 of daub. These would have needed about 300 litres per cubic metre of mortar, at least 2,600m^3, plus water for slaking the lime, a total of about 5,000m^3. This was probably carted from a nearby river: a 250kg capacity four-wheeled cart (with one driver and six mules, and two men to load and unload) would have taken 20,000 loads. At 96 minutes per cart-load, this water would have taken 32,000 man-hours. One cart could have done five trips a day, therefore 10 carts, say, would have taken 400 days. The provision of water then, was not only labour intensive, but required considerable equipment for its transport.

Timber, or charcoal, would have been needed for lime-burning, firing the tile- and brick-kilns, and for metalworking. Consumption rates and the on-site production of many of the materials are unknown, but some approximation can be made to indicate the scale of fuel provision. Some may have been waste from timber processing and carpentry.

About 12 tonnes of iron would have been needed to produce the nails in the hoard found at Inchtuthil. This would have required about 72 tonnes of ore (Cleere and Crossley, 1985), and 144 tonnes of charcoal (to smelt the ore), produced from 1,000 tonnes of timber (Cleere, 1976). Their figures suggest that providing fuel for the production of these nails would have taken about 22,000 man-hours, plus providing charcoal for ore-roasting, pre-heating furnaces, forging, and producing other ironwork. A total of 50,000 man-hours for providing fuel for the ironwork of a timber-phase fortress may not be unreasonable (though much of this would not have been on site). One oak trunk will burn one tonne of lime (Dix, 1982); about 2 tonnes of timber per tonne of lime. The 1,630m^3 of lime needed at Inchtuthil would have weighed about 1,430 tonnes, and thus required 2,860 tonnes of timber (about 2,740m^3). Tile production required 10 times the quantity of fuel (Peacock, 1982). Inchtuthil required about 366,000 *tegulae* (2,200 tonnes) and 375,000 *imbrices* (940 tonnes), firing these would therefore have needed 31,400 tonnes of timber.

Thus the timber needed to produce basic building materials for a timber-phase fortress would have been on the order of 36,260 tonnes (2,000 for ironworking; 2,860 for lime-burning; and 31,400 for tile kilns). Taking a conservative rate for felling (two man-hours per tonne), this suggests a minimum of 72,500 man-hours, excluding selecting the timber, snedding, preparing, and transporting. This excludes fuel for any lead-working, glass-making, bricks, and pipes.

Labour to manufacture materials

The main manufactured materials in a fortress were tiles, bricks and pipes, nails and other metalwork, and glass.

A timber-phase fortress probably required roof-tiles (Inchtuthil needed 366,000 *tegulae* and 375,000 *imbrices*), bricks and ducts for any hypocausts (e.g. in masonry-built bathhouse, *praetorium*, and *principia*) and pipes. It is not evident whether these were made locally (i.e. in a military kiln), or imported, perhaps from a tilery operated by the *Classis Britannica*. Tile-making was not a simple or rapid matter, but how long it took is open to considerable conjecture. It is difficult to imagine a *tegula* taking less than five minutes to mould (fill the mould, compact it, smooth the clay, and form the cut-outs). At, say, 10 *tegulae* an hour, they would have taken 36,600 man-hours just to mould. If we allow twice this rate for *imbrices*, and double the resultant moulding time to allow for preparing the clay, firing and clearing, we have a labour requirement of around 110,000 man-hours. This is a very crude estimate, and is very conservative, perhaps grossly so. A total of about 150,000 man-hours for manufacturing roof-tiles and pipes is perhaps not an unreasonable conservative estimate. This excludes building, maintaining and guarding the kilns; transporting ingredients and finished goods; and providing clay, water and fuel. It also excludes producing bricks, tiles and pipes for the bathhouse, *praetorium*, and *principia*.

Ironwork could have been made on site, from imported iron-billets, or the finished goods may have been imported, at least initially. Making nails would presumably have taken much the same time wherever it was carried out (though collecting the billets, fuel, etc. would have varied considerably with location). The main significance of the location of the nail production is not so much on transport, but on the numbers of men needed on site. (If soldiers were making nails and other ironwork they were not available for on-site construction, and had to be housed, fed, etc.)

Inchtuthil's hoard contained about 875,000 to one million nails. Nails would have weighed about 20% less than the iron-billets from which they were made. All the nails in the hoard could have been made in about 59,000 man-hours (experimental ironworking by Sim, 1998). This figure should be doubled or trebled to allow for a striker and perhaps an apprentice. This figure excludes providing fuel (charcoal), ore mining and roasting, producing the bloom and the billet, and forming it into suitably-sized bar, and the production of the equipment (furnaces, tools, hearths, etc.), and transport. Sim's experimental work, applied to Inchtuthil, suggests that forging the initial bloom (about 11 tonnes) to produce the nails would thus have taken about 5,000 man-hours. Forging the bloom into billets and then bar might have taken about 1,500 man-hours.

Allowance must be made for producing any iron door- and window-furniture. One door-pivot binding was found at Inchtuthil; there were probably over 3,000 doors. This would have been more complex and time consuming than making a large nail (30 minutes); at around three hours each, 3,000 bindings would have taken about 10,000 man-hours, perhaps considerably more. A similar figure might be suggested for other door and window furniture, but again this (and their presence) is very speculative.

These figures are only approximate (and exclude transport), but show that the effort involved in producing nails is likely to have exceeded that to produce the billets. However, there are so many unknown matters (e.g. how many nails were used? what other ironwork was required? what work-rates are reasonable?) that a firm estimate of labour for ironworking cannot be suggested with confidence. Labour for the nails might have been around 180,000 man-hours, plus perhaps a further 20,000 man-hours for door-pivot bindings, but this is very speculative.

It is not clear whether glazed-windows were rare in the timber phase (only one fragment was found at Inchtuthil). Glass might have been cast on-site, and installed after the timber buildings were first occupied. No estimate has been made of the labour involved because the extent and type of glazing is unknown, and may well have been minimal. Similarly lead-working is also excluded from the figures.

Summary of non-constructional work on-site

This chapter has outlined the types of labour necessary but not directly involved in constructional work needed on site. The suggested allowances are conjectural, but not unreasonable. These suggested that the total on-site construction labour figure should be increased by 5-10% for organisation, administration and supervision; 5% for staffing the Stores; 25% for welfare of men and animals; 25% for guarding and protection; 15% for military training; 5-10% for those unfit and injured; and 5-10% for those off-site. This suggests that the numbers of men on site might have been twice the number engaged directly in construction work. This is a very substantial number.

Table E summarises the labour that was essential to the building of a timber-phase fortress in addition to the on-site constructional labour at nearly 10.5 million man-hours. These figures exclude a variety of tasks such as setting up kilns and the quarry; producing glass, iron, and specialist and transportational tools and equipment; providing transport animals; producing foodstuffs and fodder etc. About 4.6 million man-hours of this non-constructional labour requirement was needed in the early part of the timber-phase (including 2 million for organisation, welfare and military tasks), and 5.8 million in the later stage.

Note IV: Fodder requirements during construction

Assumptions
A full-strength legion had 900 mules, 400 oxen, and 230 horses; the construction workforce perhaps had 450 mules, 200 oxen, and say 200 horses. Daily consumption: hard-fodder (i.e. grain) at 3kg per pack-animal, 7kg per ox, and 5.5kg per horse; green-fodder at 6kg per mule, 11kg per ox, and 7kg per horse (alternatively twice this amount of pasturage); and water at 21 litres per pack-animal, 19 litres per ox, and 30 litres per horse. Other foodstuffs (e.g. beans, wheat, leaves) might have been provided. The proportions of hard and green fodder or pasturage would have varied over the year. The numbers of animals might also have varied over the year. No account is taken of feed etc. for any animals kept for meat. Figures exclude the labour required to provide these foodstuffs.

Daily requirements (tonnes)
HARD FODDER: mules 1.35; oxen 1.40; horses 1.10; total: 3.85.
GREEN FODDER: mules 2.70; oxen 2.20; horses 1.40; total: 6.30.
WATER: mules 9.45; oxen 3.80; horses 6.00; total: 19.25.
DAILY TOTAL: 29.40 tonnes.

Table E Summary of non-constructional labour for a timber-phase fortress

TASK	MAN-HOURS	TASK	MAN-HOURS
ADDITIONAL LABOUR		PROVISION OF MATERIALS	
Organisation, admin and supervision	210,000	timber	569,000
		stone	56,000
stores	90,000	gravel, sand	5,000
welfare (workforce)	300,000	lime	175,000
welfare (animals etc.)	230,000	daub	10,000
guarding, protection	530,000	water	32,000
military training	320,000	tiles, etc.	150,000
unfit, injured	150,000	nails, etc.	210,000
temporarily off-site	160,000	fuel (processing)	72,000
TOTAL	2,000,000	TOTAL	1,280,000
TRANSPORTING MATERIALS	660,000	SUPPORT FOR LATER MASONRY	
TRANSPORTING FOOD etc.		additional labour	3,575,000
		provision of materials	730,000
food	65,000	transport materials	980,000
water	16,000	transport food etc.	570,000
hard fodder	175,000	TOTAL	5,855,000
green fodder	285,000	TOTAL SUPPORT:	
watering animals	125,000	initial work	4,606,000
TOTAL	666,000	later masonry	5,855,000
		(Total)	(10,461,000)

Figures are based on Inchtuthil (assuming 1,000 men, 450 mules, 200 oxen and 200 horses for 1,000 days), and are rounded for clarity. Figures exclude setting-up and maintaining quarry, kilns, and slaking-pits; producing iron-billets and glass; stacking timber; transporting non-local materials; producing/obtaining food/drink/fodder and fuel; and transporting water for bathing, latrines, workshops, maintenance, etc.; and shipping to site. The figure for stone-quarrying is very conservative.

Transporting hard fodder

The daily requirements for 450 mules, 200 oxen and 200 horses was 3.85 tonnes. For 600 days this is 2,310 tonnes, about 26 ship-loads (93,600 man-hours). For 1,000 days this is 3,850 tonnes, about 43 ship-loads (154,800 man-hours). Moving hard fodder from shipping-point to site, by pack-mule, would have taken 480 man-hours per ship-load (30 men and 300 mules for 2 days): 12,480 man-hours (plus 300 mules for 52 days) for 600 days supply, and 20,640 man-hours (plus 300 mules for 86 days) for 1,000 days supply.

Transporting green fodder

The 3,780 tonnes for 600 days (6,300 tonnes for 1,000 days) is equivalent to 42 (70) ship-loads, taking 151,200 man-hours to ship for 600 days (252,000 man-hours for 1,000 days). Moving from the shipping-point to site by pack-mule would have taken 20,160 man-hours (plus 300 mules for 84 days) for 600 days, or 33,600 man-hours (plus 300 mules for 140 days) for 1,000 days.

Note V: Tools and equipment

Finds, reliefs (including Trajan's Column), and written classical sources (e.g. Josephus, Paternus, Vegetius) show that the Romans had a great variety of tools. Each soldier probably had a saw, bucket, axe, pick, rope, sickle, and chain, and specialists must also have had specialised tools. These are suggested by archaeological evidence, common sense and traditional practice. The following lists summarise what the Romans would have used.

Carpenter and timber-worker

Adze (preliminary shaping); augers; axes (felling trees); de-barking knife?; beetle (hammer-type tool used with wedges); billhook; bradawl (pilot-holes); chisels (cutting mortices); compass and dividers (for transferring measurements); *dolabra* (combined axe and adze); draw-knife; bow-drill and bits; files (e.g. for finishing mortices); gouges; hammers (equivalent of claw-hammer, club-hammer, and sledge-hammer?); knives; mallet (tapping joints and pegs home); pinchers (e.g. for removing nails); planes; rules; saws (cutting timber to length and joint-cutting); scraper; squares; wedges (of iron, and of seasoned oak for cleaving timber). Also numerous measuring tools (including plumb- and chalk-lines, squares, mitres, compasses, bevels, levels, gauges, rules, straight-edges, and calipers), and tools for holding and gripping (holdfasts, clamps, hook-pins).

Mason and quarry-man

Chisels (a masonry chisel is blunter than a wood-working chisel; there are numerous types); hammers (probably several different sizes); levers; mallets; pick-axe; rules; spades; iron-wedges. Tools for measuring: graduated rule (*regula*); several types of squares (*normae*) including the plumb level (*libella*); plumb line (*perpendiculum*); compass (*circinus*); *groma* (for right-angles); a level (*chorobates*) might have been used for masonry.

Plasterer/renderer

Floats; hawk (to allow the plasterer to hold a quantity of mortar as he works); scraper (for keying wet plaster/render); spot-boards; trowels; mixing/transporting troughs.

Labourer, turf-cutter, and earth-worker

Profile? (to gauge the slope of a rampart or ditch); rule; measuring-rod or pattern (e.g. to establish the standard size of a turf); scythe; shovel (*rutrum*); spade (*pala*); turf-cutter (*ligo*).

Equipment and plant

Amphorae? (with necks broken off, for containing wet materials such as lime); baskets (for moving earth, gravel etc.); carpenter's bench; carpenter's horses; gloves? (for masons and quarrymen); grindstones; timbers (e.g. baulks used as crude work-benches, for temporary support, as levers, as rollers); trestles; troughs (for containing wet materials). Rope (e.g. for securing turfs to carrier's back; guiding fall of trees during felling and for making drags; for hoisting; for forming scaffolding; etc.) was probably hemp or similar, but leather might have been used for some tasks; a variety of thicknesses and lengths likely. Ropes (or chains) marked to fixed lengths may have been used for measuring. Scaffolding, working platforms and ladders would have been of timber, probably small-diameter trunks lashed together with rope, leather or sinew. Other access and erection equipment would be based on simple components: ropes, levers, wooden blocks and pulleys. Lifting equipment may have included pulleys (*orbiculus*); winches (*sucula*); a pulley-and-winch crane (*rechanum*); blocks-and-tackle, hooks, and lewis-bolts (to hoist large masonry stones).

8 Transport of supplies on-site and to site

The transportation of building materials, equipment, food and fodder required a substantial amount of labour and transport equipment and needs to be considered in detail. However, the assessment of the labour and plant needed to transport materials and equipment is more speculative and tenuous than that for the construction-work because there is virtually no direct evidence, and the number of plausible options is vast. Likely methods, and their significance, are identified and discussed in this chapter. Transport has been considered under two headings: transportation of materials and equipment to the fortress site, and transportation within the fortress area. This division allows the significance of variations (e.g. to modes of transport) to be considered, and separates on-site labour from off-site labour.

On-site transport of materials and equipment, food and fodder

Transportation assumptions
Common sense suggests that most building materials and heavy equipment would have been kept in a main storage area or areas, from which they would have been moved to the building sites as needed. In most cases it is not possible to say which on-site transport method was the most likely. It was not necessarily the most efficient (in terms of man-hours), speed may have been more important, or perhaps a combination of transport methods was used, or varied, according to what was available at any one time.

Some materials (e.g. nails?) were probably stored in specialist or more secure stores. Heavy and bulky items (e.g. gateway posts; wattles) and some locally produced materials (e.g. tiles) may have gone direct to the site of each building. To reduce transport (mileage, effort, handling, use of equipment) all locally obtained materials may have been treated in this way, with processing (e.g. timber preparation) at or near to their source. Some materials (e.g. water) may not have been stored at all, but collected as needed. Where large quantities of a material (e.g. wall-post timbers, or shingles) were needed it is likely that there was some temporary stockpiling, to act as a buffer for balancing supply and demand.

Handling is difficult to define or assess with any precision. It includes loading and unloading, stacking in temporary stockpiles, and any short-distance transporting to facilitate these. It also includes moving materials about during preparation and placing work (e.g. turning over a tie-beam during joint-cutting, or stacking *tegulae* on a roof ready for the tiler). Many of these handling jobs could have been minor matters if the construction work was well organised (largely included for in the work-rates), though moving very heavy items would have been labour intensive. Much depends on how much the builders could work in accordance with experience and initiative.

We do not know how components were raised and positioned. Smaller components were probably carried up ladders, or pulled up in baskets. Large timbers could have been carried, or shuffled-up by a few men with ropes and temporary wedges, or hoisted with ropes or simple crane arrangements. Simplicity, of operation and equipment, is likely.

Man-carrying was probably the basic on-site transportation method because, in theory, almost all materials could have been carried (using baskets etc. where necessary; the few very large timbers could have been man-hauled). Man-carrying is very flexible in terms of routeways and the number of men involved, and needs little equipment, preparation, or skill. However, some awkwardly shaped or non-solid materials do not lend themselves to man-carrying. It is therefore necessary to identify which materials are most likely to have been moved by cart or pack-animal, and the significance of these alternatives on overall man-hours, task duration, waiting-time and team arrangements, and the implications for additional equipment and its care.

The most plausible alternatives to man-carrying are sleds and ropes, carts and wagons, pack-animals, and water-borne transport (ships, and perhaps river-barges). Timbers (tree-trunks or prepared timbers) could have been moved on sleds (timber platforms, hauling by men or draught-animals) with or without timber 'roadways'. Tree-trunks could have been hauled along the ground, but this would have damaged prepared timbers. Carts and wagons could have moved unit materials (e.g. tiles), bulk materials (e.g. sand), liquids (e.g. water or lime, in suitable containers), and most timbers. Even very large timbers could have been moved by purpose-made wagons. Pack-animals could have moved the smaller timbers (e.g. wattles; wall-bracings; planking), unit materials, and liquids. Carts and wagons would have needed roads (which may have been provided early for this reason). The Inchtuthil iron-hoard included nine used cart-tyres, and many streets had tyre-ruts, but this is insufficient to indicate cart type, what was carried, where from or to, or with what frequency.

Assumptions about the transport of food to site are summarised in **Note VI**.

Modes of transport

While the inherent flexibility of man-carrying makes it the most likely way of moving most materials on site, some use of carts, wagons, and pack-animals is probable. A nominal maximum man-carrying load of 50kg has been assumed. As this is a heavy load, except for short journeys, it could be argued that the time allowed for collecting materials from stores should be increased (say by 25%) to allow for a reduced load per man, or for resting-time between carries. Nevertheless, a load of 50kg (110lb) for well-trained, fit and experienced men is not implausible, and many loads would have been lighter (i.e. where materials did not weigh multiples of 50kg, or were bulky).

Likely travel-distances for Inchtuthil were approximated, based on the straight-line routes between the stores and the sites of the individual buildings, and converted to a time (based on a travel rate of 1m every 1.3 seconds). If the travel-routes used the fortress streets, on-site transport would have taken longer. For example, the street route between Inchtuthil's stores and the most distant building (barrack XXXVII) was about 26% longer than the straight-line route (twice 830m, taking about 36 minutes, compared to about 29 minutes for the straight-line route). The street route to the nearest building (barrack XIII) would have taken 7% longer. Therefore, there is an argument for increasing the collect component of the man-hour requirements by about 25%, to allow for lighter loads, and by about 15% to allow for routes using the streets.

What would have been the significance of moving materials by cart instead of by man-carrying? Take the example of the main-timbers of Inchtuthil's barracks XVII (32,100kg). Dividing this by 50kg gives 642 man-loads but in fact 724 man-loads would have been needed because the timbers do not divide conveniently into 50kg loads (this is an 'extra' 82 loads, about 16%). This timber could have been moved by one large ox-cart in 137 man-hours, a two-wheeler in 130 man-hours, or by man-carrying in 181 man-hours. However, man-carrying is theoretically less labour intensive if provision and care of the carts and animals is included. The duration of the task, and the equipment available, are also relevant: 51 hours for the ox-cart (30 hours for two carts), 76 hours for the two-wheeler (38 hours for two), and 90.5 hours by a team of two men (42.5 hours for two teams).

This is a simplistic analysis, and small variations in assumptions can significantly affect the conclusions. However, on balance, man-carrying was perhaps the most likely option as it required less equipment, little preparation or care, was simpler to organise, and was flexible.

Pack-animals were probably used. The main-timbers would not have been suitable for mules and donkeys (a 117kg (260lb) barracks wall-post was too heavy; a 65kg (143lb) partition wall-post is theoretically half a mule-load, but would have been too long and awkward). Planking and wattles could have been carried by pack-animals (they would have been awkward loads for man-carrying). Consider the implications of moving the external-cladding timbers for a barracks: they could have been moved by two men in 89 hours (178 man-hours), or by 20 mules and five men in 97 hours (484 man-hours). (Mules have a considerable advantage over donkeys, not only can they carry twice the load, they require considerably less attendance on the journey.) Man-carrying therefore seems more likely, though if pack-animals (or carts and wagons) were on-site and otherwise idle they would probably have been used. In practice there were probably a combination of methods.

Earth-moving is shown on Trajan's column, but we do not know whether legionaries used baskets for moving bulk-goods over long distances. A comparison between moving a notional 10m^3 of gravel/sub-soil 500m and 1,000m by man-carrying with baskets (25kg or 55lb loads), ox-carts (750kg or 1,650lb), small mule-carts (100kg or 220lb), pack-donkey (70kg or 155lb), and pack-mules (140kg or 310lb) shows that large carts are theoretically more efficient. However, this excludes provision of carts, and preparation and care of their equipment, their draught-animals, and the roads, all labour intensive. (Experimental work by the Royal School of Military Engineering suggests that a very basic tactical road would have taken 40 man-hours to build over grassland, 450 man-hours over heathland, and 600 man-hours over forest, per 100m.)

Much of the on-site bulk-goods were produced in small quantities, widely spread and a little at a time (e.g. spoil from wall-post trenches), and needed moving only a short distance, all making man-carrying more practical. The further the distance travelled the more unrealistic man-carrying becomes, but the reverse is true for pack-animals. Pack-animals also have the advantage of not needing a prepared surface, simply the clearing of any dense vegetation, and are likely where material sources were distant and/or surfaced roads impractical. Carts were probably only used where large quantities came moderate distances and where road provision was realistic.

Transporting supplies to site

Work-rates, equipment and handling

These approximate labour calculations exclude the labour involved in providing the transport equipment itself. The intention is simply to provide an approximation of the scale of magnitude of the effort involved in moving supplies to site. This allows the on-site construction labour to be put into context.

Roman transportation methods, load capacities, rates, and duration of travel, including discussion of the evidence, are well covered in the literature (summarised in Shirley, 2000); the rates suggested below are based on them. There is obviously a trade-off between the load and the rate of travel and the duration of travel, so it is not possible to give firm figures for any of these. The transport rates, which exclude allowance for adverse weather or ground conditions or undue urgency, are: a donkey (or pony?) with a 75kg (165lb) load travelled at 4km/hr (24km/day), and a mule (or horse?) with a 150kg (330lb) load, at 6km/hr (36km/day). A large ox-cart, with a 750kg (1,650lb) load and with 6 oxen travelled at 3km/hr (24km/day), and a small ox-cart, with a 500kg (1,100lb) load and 4 oxen, at 3km/hr (or 24km/day). A four-wheeled cart, with 250kg (550lb) load and 6 mules, travelled at 7km/hr (36km/day), and a two-wheeled cart, with 100kg (220lb) load and 3 mules, at 8km/hr (40km/day). Each cart or wagon, would have needed a driver, plus 2 men to load and unload. Water transport (as Pearson, 1995) included 45 tonne (55m^3) river-barges moving at 1.85km/hr, and coastal vessels of 90 tonnes at 5.5km/hr, each with a crew of three.

It is unlikely that ships and barges (and perhaps any extra provision of carts, wagons and pack-animals) would have been provided specifically for transporting supplies to the site of any one fortress, at least during the timber-phase. They would have been costly to provide, in time (man-hours and duration) and in monetary terms (whether purchase, or cash-equivalents). The more expensive items (i.e. ships) are likely to have expended less of their working life transporting supplies to one fortress than the less expensive (i.e. pack-donkey).

It is not realistic here to try to quantify the labour inputs necessary to build ships, make carts, or breed animals, but the range of tasks must be considered. For example, ships and barges had to be designed, materials obtained and transported, construction work undertaken, and tested. This would have involved a variety of different skilled workmen, all of whom had to be organised and paid (and/or fed, clothed, and housed). Part or all of this work may have been undertaken by the military themselves, or obtained from civilians (by purchase, extortion, coercion, taxation, etc.). It is also possible that finished vessels, vehicles, or animals were obtained (or hired?) directly from civilians. But whether the man who built the ship (or grew the grain to feed him) was a soldier, civilian, or slave, his labour still involved costs.

Ships and barges would have needed sails, ropes, pulleys and blocks, oars, etc., and these items would have had a relatively short life compared with that of the vessel. The vessel would also have needed routine maintenance, cyclic repair, and repair or replacement following any accidents. Similarly with carts and wagons, pack- and draught-animals would have needed harnesses, ropes, panniers, etc. All these sundries would have themselves required maintenance and repair, and eventual replacement. We do not know how goods were transported to site, or where they came from; the calculation of off-site transport can thus be only very tentative. It seems reasonable to assume that supplies brought from a great distance would have travelled by sea and river, but this is not necessarily so.

After transferring goods from sea-going vessels, the remainder of the journey might have been made by barge and/or pack-animal, cart/wagon or man-carrying. Water transport is not necessarily the best option, since much depends on what inputs are included. For example, it may have been more economic to provide a string of pack-animals than a barge or wagon, depending on what proportion of the costs of providing the vessel, training the crew, straightening and dredging the river etc., or building, protecting and maintaining the road is included. The duration of the journeys may, or may not, have been relevant. Reliability, or season, might have been important (e.g. pack-animals could have travelled over rougher terrain than wagons, and for more of the year than ships).

Where materials were needed in large quantities and were available locally from a single source (e.g. stone?), it would probably have been economic to build a road for carts or wagons. But where sources were more distant pack-animals might have been more efficient, and scattered local materials might have been collected efficiently by man-carrying. Also, we do not know whether transport choices were limited by availability of manpower or transport equipment, or the season, or variations in supply requirements, or whether speed was more important than efficiency.

Some materials, because of their bulk, weight or fragility, probably went straight to the building where they were to be used, though this is somewhat speculative. The most likely materials here are the heavier timbers (less than 4% of the total) and locally made roof-tiles. The transport distances assumed for local materials are only approximate (say to the nearest half-kilometre), so variations in the location of storage areas are effectively irrelevant. Storage areas would have needed preparation (defences? surfacing? clearance of vegetation?) and staffing.

It is also relevant to consider how many times materials might have been handled (loaded, moved, unloaded, stacked, counted, recorded) before going to the building sites. Unnecessary handling could have been introduced if, for example, materials were delivered far in advance of their use, which may have been necessary to allow for seasonal restrictions on production or transport. Even with a sophisticated and organised supply system some inefficiencies must have occurred due to unforeseeable or uncontrollable events, such as severe weather, accidents or attack.

Comparison of the different transport methods shows that they would have taken very different amounts of time and labour to move the local main materials. In practice, of course, it is unlikely that only one method would have been used, but this comparison does show the significance of the type of transport on resources and task duration. The methods compared are pack-donkeys (75kg or 165lb loads), pack-mules (150kg or 330lb), small carts (100kg or 220lb), large carts (250kg or 550lb), small wagons (500kg or 1,100lb) and large wagons (750kg or 1,650lb). These needed varying amounts of draught-animals and attendance. Small carts had 3 mules, large carts 6, small wagons had 4 oxen and large wagons 6. One man was needed for 3 donkeys or 20 mules, each cart and wagon needed a driver, and 2 men for loading and unloading (when driver and animals were resting/maintaining equipment, feeding etc.). Loading/unloading times would have varied too, with donkeys and small carts taking 20 man-minutes, mules and large carts 30, small wagons 45 and large wagons 60 man-minutes.

The main materials could have been moved by 990,000 pack-donkey trips, taking 640,000 man-hours and 1,080,000 donkey-hours. Mules would have taken 490,000 trips, 270,000 man-hours and 430,000 mule-hours. The 730,000 small-cart trips would have taken 660,000 man-hours and 1,610,000 mule-hours, the 300,000 large-cart trips 330,000 man-hours and 1,550,000 mule-hours. For the small and large wagons the figures are 150,000 and 100,000 trips, 250,000 and 190,000 man-hours, and 770,000 and 850,000 oxen-hours. A small cart would thus appear to have little advantage over pack-mules, and a 250kg (550lb) cart would appear more useful than a 100kg (220lb) cart: for a given load the animal-hours are similar, but the man-hours are about half. Much depends on the actual conditions: loading and unloading may have taken longer, loads may have had to be lighter, travelling conditions may have been poor (which would have significantly increased travel-time). These figures also exclude providing the transport equipment, welfare, maintenance/repair, and organisation/supervision/administration, and any accidents or attacks. However, theoretically at least, the heavier main materials (50% main-timbers; stone) could, for example, have been moved by 70 large wagons in 167 working-days. The remaining main materials could, for example, have been moved by 900 pack-mules in 19 working-days.

In practice though the situation was probably more complex than just total man-hours. Availability of men and equipment, the season, and the terrain, are likely to have been relevant, and although the mule could carry 150kg, the load had to be divided and balanced. A prime advantage of pack-animals is that they can travel over rough ground, and are thus suited to materials that are relatively scattered, or where roads would be difficult to build. They could have carried the smaller timbers, roof-tiles and shingles. The advantage of carts and wagons is that they need less manpower to maintain them (the feed and water demands of pack-animals would have been considerable), and can carry heavier loads. Their main disadvantage is the need for roads, and each would have required a driver (a mule-train of 20, moving three tonnes, would have needed one driver; but this load, if moved at one time, by 750kg or 1,650lb wagons would have needed four drivers).

It is likely that the fortress builders used whatever transport methods were available, taking into account variations in supply demands, the season and weather conditions, and variations in available manpower and transport equipment. It is probable that the legion arrived with at least, and perhaps significantly more than, its usual provision of pack-animals and vehicles, and these would probably not have been idle.

The main materials for a timber-phase fortress (excluding masonry) could have been moved in about three weeks, excluding preparing the transport routes, which in the case of roads for wagons could have been considerable. A large wagon could have moved the stone used at Inchtuthil in about 148 days (but only about 6% of this stone would have been needed in the first season). A quarter of a legions presumed usual transport provision could have moved the main materials to site from local sources, or from where ships were unloaded.

Movement of non-local materials

Assessing the labour involved in moving non-local materials is even more tenuous as we do not know what was imported, from where, or how it was moved. However, some rough estimates may be attempted. The most likely building materials not available locally are very large timbers, glass, iron (either billets or finished goods) and iron-tools, and any specialist equipment. These were probably imported by sea and river, and then by cart, wagon or pack-animal. The large timbers might have been hauled, though not over large distances.

Moving these items would have been a significant task, but these items were probably not needed in large quantities. Not only would these items have come a long way, they had to arrive when (or before) needed. The organisation and administrative effort would have been considerable: the quantities of materials, and when they were needed, had to be assessed, then obtained, and moved to site. Other than the estimating, this may not have directly involved on-site personnel; there may have been some form of central supply system. If there was none, then the task would have been considerably more formidable.

For the fortress buildings at Inchtuthil there were about 2,200 timbers over 500kg (1,100lb) (e.g. a barracks tie-beam weighed about 620kg, or 1,370lb); these would have weighed about 1,500 tonnes, about 9% of the total weight of the main-timbers. Of these only 300 would have weighed 750-1,000kg (1,650-2,200lb) (each of the four gateways had 18 main uprights, each weighing about 940kg). If wagons were used for moving timbers, special arrangements would have had to be made for only about 4%. Thus most of the timbers could have been moved relatively easily, given some form of surfaced roadway. If the *principia* basilica nave-posts and tie-beams, and *Fabrica* tie-beams (together about 120 tonnes) were not available locally, they could have been one load for a coastal vessel.

The 12 tonnes of iron-billets needed to produce the nails in the Inchtuthil hoard could have been carried in 24 carts (500kg or 1,100lb capacity) or 80 pack-mule loads, and have been about 13% of the load of a coastal vessel.

Establishing and protecting supply routes

This is another area where labour inputs cannot realistically be calculated, but it is possible to point to the type of activity that may have been necessary. Presumably only the local routes were the responsibility of the on-site workforce, but the labour for establishing and protecting non-local supply routes must be considered. We do not know how much guarding was necessary. Materials moved, locally and non-locally, may, in some areas at least, have needed very little protection, though high-valued materials (e.g. iron) probably would have done.

Supply routes had to be determined, both in overall strategic terms and in detail on the ground, and built. In areas of low vegetation this might have been little more than marking out a route for pack-animals, or using some established pathways. However, it could have involved clearing forest and constructing roads suitable for heavy wagons. Some of these routeways may have been intended to be part of a permanent road network, and thus not strictly exclusive to the fortress-building effort.

Note VI: Transporting food to site

Assumed method for Inchtuthil

The basic daily ration of 1.4kg/man/day, was imported by small (90 tonne) coastal-vessels, each with a crew of three. Travelling at about 50km/day one round-trip would have taken about 6 weeks (3 men for 42 x 24-hour days: 3,000 man-hours). It would have taken about 300 man-hours to load and unload each ship. Provisions were transferred to pack-mules (capacity 150kg), working in trains of 20 mules. The travel distance from shipping point to site was about 15-18km, a round-trip equivalent to the daily travel-distance of a pack-mule. Ships may have arrived singly, or in convoy, with goods moved to site rapidly (for protection from the weather, and to allow ships to return). Coastal shipping would not have operated all year; if limited to about 25 weeks, at least two vessels would have been needed. The grain component (about 60% of the foodstuffs total) was, for tactical reasons, probably delivered early in the construction period. Thus deliveries were probably not evenly spaced.

Shipping basic foodstuffs to site

600 DAYS SUPPLY FOR 1,000 MEN: 840 tonnes (10 ship-loads) would have taken 3,000 man-hours to load and to unload, and 15,000 to ship, a total of 36,000 man-hours. 1,000 DAYS SUPPLY FOR 1,000 MEN: 1,400 tonnes (16 ship-loads) would have taken 4,800 man-hours to load and unload, and 24,000 to ship, a total of 57,600 man-hours.

Mule-training foodstuffs (from shipping-point to site)

Each ship-load is equivalent to 600 mule-loads (30 trains of 20 mules). If the goods were moved in 2 days, 15 trains would have been needed (300 mules, plus 15 drivers). At 2 men each for 10 minutes to load a mule, it would have taken 3.33 hours (6.66 man-hours) to load the train; 10 men would have taken 5 hours to load all 15 trains. Thus, per ship-load, allow 2 days for 300 mules, 15 drivers, 10 loaders, and 5 unloaders (there would have been some lost waiting and travelling time), say 480 man-hours.
600 DAYS SUPPLY FOR 1,000 MEN (10 ship-loads): 4,800 man-hours plus 300 mules for 20 days.
1,000 DAYS SUPPLY FOR 1,000 MEN (16 ship-loads): 7,680 man-hours plus 300 mules for 32 days.

Water

Probably transported in barrels, say 250kg capacity four-wheeled carts each pulled by 6 mules. At 2.5 litres/man, 1,000 men required 2,500 litres per day (2.5 tonnes), say 10 cart-loads. With a round-trip of 1km, two carts (each with one driver and 6 mules) could have delivered this water each day, assuming they worked in pairs to load and unload the barrels. The daily requirement is thus 16 man-hours, plus 2 carts and 12 mules. 600 DAYS WATER FOR 1,000 MEN: 9,600 man-hours, plus 12 mules for 600 days. 1,000 DAYS WATER FOR 1,000 MEN: 16,000 man-hours, plus 12 mules for 1,000 days.

Summary

It thus took about 50,000 man-hours to transport (including loading and unloading) basic foodstuffs and water for 1,000 men for 600 days (80,000 man-hours for 1,000 men for 1,000 days).

These approximations are for basic provisions only and exclude providing transport-equipment, food/fodder/water for the transport teams, maintenance and repairs, and preparation or protection of routeways and trans-shipment areas. There are numerous other plausible transport methods and routes.

9 The labour force and the construction period

This chapter considers how many men were needed to build a fortress, and how long it would have taken. How might the work have been programmed, and would it have been feasible for a team of constant size to have built the fortress as a continuous building operation? There is no way of knowing whether the workforce was constant (either in size or composition) or whether work was seasonal, but suggesting simple programmes can illustrate a range of possibilities that fit with the evidence and common sense, and indicate the complexity of the issue.

The skills and composition of the labour force

Roman military treatises suggest that training and practice were ongoing, but we do not know at what rate it would have continued during full-scale construction work. In addition to military training and practice the non-constructional duties would have included guarding (both of the construction site and the supply routes), those affected by injury or ill-health, those engaged in organisation and administration, and time taken to maintain weaponry and equipment. The amount of time that any of these tasks took is likely to have varied, in the short and the long term, in response to normal rotas, the progress of the construction work, the season, and outside influences.

The distinction between military and welfare labour is not clear-cut. Some nominally military tasks (e.g. polishing *lornica*?) may have been carried out by non-combatants, and many nominally welfare tasks (e.g. food preparation?) may have been carried out by soldiers. The concern here is not so much with who did what, as with how long it all took. A difficulty here is to distinguish what was extra because of the construction work, and to assess whether this distinction is relevant. A soldier, for example, needed feeding whether he was training, campaigning, or building. However, if we are considering the full labour implications of building a fortress we must allow for feeding the workforce.

Few of the construction tasks, particularly during the timber phase, would have required significant skill or experience. Few of the carpentry or masonry tasks were highly skilled, requiring instead only disciplined and motivated men with common sense and a general practical ability. Most of the work would not have required much breadth of experience or ability, nor need most of it have been carried out to a good standard. Some specialists would have been needed, to carry out the few critical tasks (e.g. initial setting-out, cutting rafter-tenons) and to supervise. Even skills needed to produce building materials (e.g. nail-making, glass manufacture) are in themselves straightforward craft skills, requiring depth but not breadth of experience. There is evidence (e.g. from Paternus, Vegetius, and from Vindolanda) that legions had a wide range of specialists (e.g. architects, surveyors, wood-cutters and stone-cutters, tile-makers and shinglers, lime-burners, smiths and plumbers, and plasterers).

The regularity of military building perhaps biases us to think that it was the result of efficient organisation, when it may, in fact, have been staid, inefficient, inflexible, and haphazard. The entire construction process may have had to follow materials availability, rather than direct it. The most onerous tasks were not the construction work but its organisation. Estimating the quantities of the various materials, and getting them to site, in sensible amounts and sequences, would have been a very considerable task. But this assumes that it was done efficiently, which need not have been the case. For example, it would have been self-evident that the fortress would need many workmen (there may have been a standard size for a fortress-building contingent), and vast amounts of timber, tiles, etc. Perhaps most materials were simply produced, and to some extent stockpiled, until the work neared completion and further supplies were halted, with consequent fluctuations in supply causing delays and wastage. Materials may have been supplied at a rate determined by what was available, or what transport was possible. Items may have been delivered to site without calculation of actual need. Production, transport and on-site storage may have been chaotic and inefficient.

The origin of the workforce may have influenced labour requirements because some types of people would have worked more effectively, or for longer hours, than others. A legionary soldier, for example, was probably the most effective, being well-disciplined, trained, strong, well-fed, and with medical care. Civilians (perhaps involved in the extraction, processing or manufacturing of materials, or transport) could have been equally efficient, with profit or coercion substituting for military discipline, and for some specialised tasks may have been more so. Women (and children) could have been as effective as men where physical strength was not critical (e.g. mule-handling, charcoal burning?). Specialist labour (e.g. wall-painters, mosaic-layers), perhaps employed privately by officers, is also likely to have been efficient. The efficiency of any non-free workforce is very difficult to assess. In theory they could have been as efficient (though presumably would have needed some degree of over-seeing), but this assumes that they were as healthy and well-trained as legionaries (perhaps unlikely) and motivated (if for different reasons).

Some on-site welfare tasks may have been carried out by non-military personnel. Also, some personal servants or dependants (e.g. officers' wives and children, hostages?) may have made no contribution to the welfare of the legion, but would have needed feeding, clothing and housing. This balance of contribution and burden is difficult to clarify, but it is probable that a legion in a frontier zone would not have carried many servants and dependants, but an established fortress undergoing rebuilding might have housed considerable proportion of 'non-productive' people.

The most skilled tasks during the timber-phase were those carried out by the planners, the carpenters and masons, and to a lesser extent the roofers. The division between skilled and unskilled is too simplistic: many labouring tasks require experience and understanding, and many skilled tasks require a very limited breadth of experience (e.g.

fixing wall-cladding would have been a simple carpentry task, cutting the rafter-feet tenons a highly skilled one). Most of the building tasks could have been learned in a short time (certainly whilst building one fortress), requiring common sense, physical fitness, and disciplined working rather than years of training.

The size of the labour force and the construction period

Numbers of men and the construction period

How many men were needed to build a new fortress? This is one of the most difficult questions to answer, but it is possible to indicate the likely scale of the workforce. We cannot assess the size of the workforce by dividing the total man-hours by the theoretical construction period. Similarly we cannot argue for the construction period by dividing the total man-hours by, say, the number of men in a legion. These crude approaches can, however, have some value in indicating whether the suggested figures are remotely plausible.

It is perhaps unlikely that the same number of men were involved each day. Variations were likely in both the demand and supply of labour and materials, and these would vary seasonally, according to the stage of construction, and in response to external factors. It is very difficult to indicate the likely significance of these variables. It would have been theoretically possible for a full legion to have constructed a fortress, and for them to have been fully employed (say 2,500 on support work, 500 on defences, and 2,000 on construction, with variations to suit the phases of the construction) but this would not have been efficient.

We do not know how the demands of fortress building and campaigning were balanced, whether the building work proceeded irrespective of the season, or whether it had to fit in with the military timetable. Construction work could have been severely restricted if most of the legion was engaged in campaigning during the late spring and summer, but it is unlikely that the site would have been completely abandoned during the campaigning period. It may be that there was a greater proportion of the legion engaged in construction during the winter, but the reverse is also possible.

From a construction, rather than a military viewpoint, building work could have proceeded all year round. Only tasks involving mortar or daub, and perhaps brick- and tile-making, could not have been carried out all year (these cannot be done in frosty conditions). Digging trenches (or excavating gravel etc.) would have been slow in frozen ground, but not impossible. Carpentry could have been carried out in temperatures below freezing, but with some loss of efficiency. Falling snow, heavy rainfall and high winds would have hampered or prevented working, but heavy falls of snow could have been cleared from working areas (though this would have taken time). Other tasks would have been better carried out at certain times of the year. Turf-working, for example, would have been difficult in very dry or wet ground, and impractical in frozen ground, and was thus probably limited to the spring and autumn.

Transport of materials would also have been affected by the weather. Land transport might have been difficult during prolonged wet weather, but easier in winter, with frozen ground easier going than mud, and sea-transport would not have been feasible during much of the winter.

Possible programme for a timber-phase fortress

Labour requirements have been estimated at 2.4 and 3.6 million man-hours for early and later on-site construction work, a further 4.6 and 5.9 million for necessary non-constructional work, plus non-local production of foodstuffs and animal fodder, tools and equipment.

The fact that Inchtuthil's camp II was initially large and then scaled down in size might suggest that the labour force was initially high, and then reduced, perhaps in a second season. However, camp II was large enough for four legions, and camp III a full legion. This is too large for a construction workforce, unless we assume either an unrealistically massive guarding and protection requirement, and/or a very much greater labour input for local transportation. There is also a practical upper limit on the number of men that could work on any task. Camp II may have been a winter or temporary campaign quarters, and its occupation may not have coincided with the construction work. Also, the camp may have been reduced in size because some men moved into the newly built barracks.

The two phases in the officers' temporary camp, the reduction in the size of camp II, and the replacing of the turf-rampart with stone, suggest (but do not prove) that Inchtuthil was built in two seasons. The occupation has been estimated at less than two years (say about 600 days) or up to about 1,000 days. The campaigning season was traditionally mid-May to mid-August, say about 14 weeks. It is thus theoretically possible that the building season could have been 38 weeks less allowance for any campaign preparation. However, this assumes that the fortress would have been built by a full legion (the labour requirements do not justify this), and that a full legion went on campaign.

A workforce of about 1,000 men (say 20% of a legion) could have built a timber fortress, but not in two seasons. If we assume a building season of about 30 weeks, then 2,000 men would have been needed over the two seasons. (This begs the question of what the rest of the legion were doing; they might have all been on-site, engaged in normal winter training, or building associated auxiliary forts.) Alternatively the fortress might have been built by a constant-sized workforce (say 1,000 men) over a constant building period (i.e. seconded to construction work and not engaged in summer campaigning). This is the simplest arrangement, and will be used for the initial consideration of possible programmes. The significance of variations can then be seen.

The total labour requirement for Inchtuthil's early work (i.e. the timber-phase excluding the later timber-phase masonry) was 7 million man-hours, and the construction period was between about 600 and 1,000 days. The construction (not allowing for inefficiencies due to teamwork and day-length, and assuming an eight-hour effective working day) could therefore have been carried out by 1,466 men working for 600 days, or 880 men working for 1,000 days (or 1,000 men for 880 days). A timber fortress workforce of about 880 to 1,465 men is thus plausible.

Of these men, the construction workers might have numbered between about 530 men (over 600 days) and 320 men (over 1,000 days). Figure **44** shows that 530 men could have carried out the on-site construction work in 600 days (88 weeks), given necessary

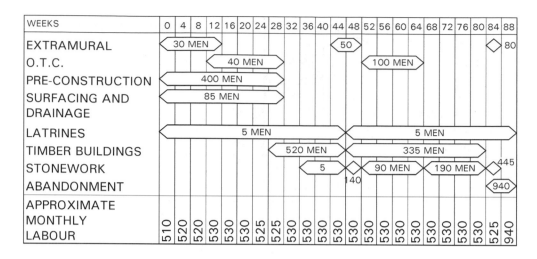

WEEKS	0	4	8	12	16	20	24	28	32	36	40	44	48	52	56	60	64	68	72	76	80	84	88
EXTRAMURAL		30 MEN										50				100 MEN							80
O.T.C.				40 MEN											100 MEN								
PRE-CONSTRUCTION			400 MEN																				
SURFACING AND DRAINAGE			85 MEN																				
LATRINES				5 MEN										5 MEN									
TIMBER BUILDINGS							520 MEN							335 MEN									
STONEWORK									5						90 MEN			190 MEN					445
ABANDONMENT											140												940
APPROXIMATE MONTHLY LABOUR	510	520	520	530	530	530	525	525	530	530	530	530	530	530	530	530	530	530	530	530	530	525	940

44 Simplified work-programme for on-site construction

support and no inefficiencies. It also shows that two seasons were required to complete the work, although there need not have been any pause. Figure **45** shows a more detailed possible programme for the first half of the work (this time using 540 on-site workmen).

The main tasks in the first half of the construction period were the rampart, ditch and counter-scarp bank, and some of the timber buildings, and in the second season the remaining buildings and stone defensive-wall. The order in which these were built, and the way the labour was divided between them is unknowable; but the figures show, in simplified terms, how it could have been done. These simple programmes take no account of external or seasonal factors, which in practice would have affected the work. Only some of this disruption could have been predicted and planned for.

The range of possible programmes is vast. In practice it is unlikely that the Roman army had developed an optimum planning and organisation method, so some planning inefficiencies are likely (they need not have been great; they may have been massive). It is likely that any planned programme, however sophisticated, would have been modified on a day-to-day basis to allow for variations in the numbers of men available, supply of materials, weather, and the progress of the construction.

Figure **46** is the simplified possible programme for the non-constructional labour at Inchtuthil. Most of the labour demands would have been constant from month to month (e.g. welfare), providing the size of the workforce were constant. This programme gives a rough idea of how many men would have been engaged in these tasks. There are problems though. While some of these tasks would have been constant, others are likely to have required more men at the start of the period than later on (for example guarding might have been more onerous before the rampart was built). In order to provide the labour for these initial tasks men must have been taken off other tasks.

There would probably have been some movement of personnel between these main tasks (military training for example is likely to have been organised on a rota basis).

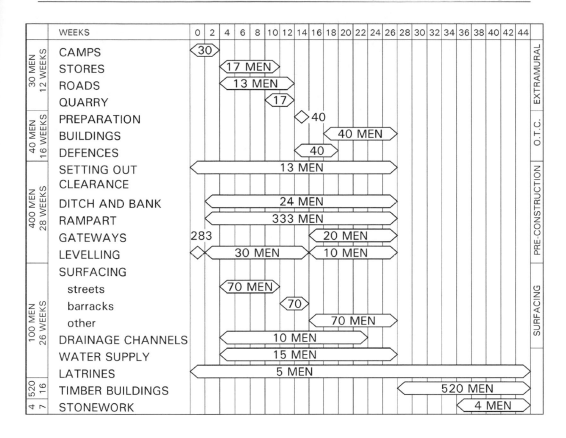

45 *Work-programme for first-half of the on-site construction*

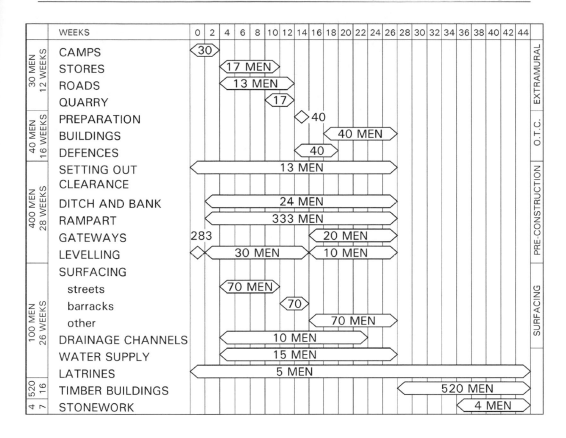

46 *Work-programme for non-constructional labour*

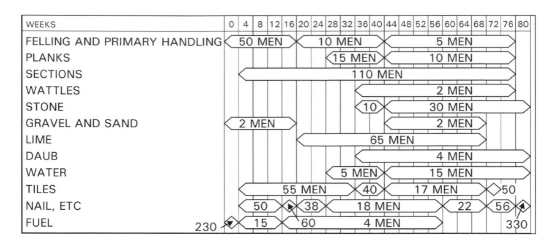

WEEKS	0	4	8	12	16	20	24	28	32	36	40	44	48	52	56	60	64	68	72	76	80
FELLING AND PRIMARY HANDLING	50 MEN					10 MEN						5 MEN									
PLANKS							15 MEN				10 MEN										
SECTIONS				110 MEN																	
WATTLES										2 MEN											
STONE										10	30 MEN										
GRAVEL AND SAND		2 MEN								2 MEN											
LIME							65 MEN														
DAUB										4 MEN											
WATER							5 MEN		15 MEN												
TILES				55 MEN				40	17 MEN					50							
NAIL, ETC		50	38	18 MEN				22	56												
FUEL	230	15	60	4 MEN					330												

47 Work-programme for the preparation of building materials

Movements between construction and non-construction tasks is also likely, including the numbers of men engaged in each. Initially more men are likely to have been engaged in the non-construction tasks (e.g. provision of materials), and less so in the later period. These movements need not have affected the number of men at Inchtuthil. Figure **47** shows how the labour for provision of materials at Inchtuthil might have been allocated, while figure **46** shows 282 men for 80 weeks, which is the theoretical requirement. Figure **47** also shows that, in practice, this is not quite enough men: the manufacture of some of the tiles and nails would have been too late. To overcome this, men could have been borrowed from the on-site workforce towards the beginning of the construction period. Alternatively, if nails were imported and not made on site, allocation of on-site labour would have been eased considerably.

Labour requirements throughout the construction period
The number of men on-site may or may not have varied over the construction period. If the work was seasonal, the numbers must have been considerable during the building season, with at least a skeleton force (for defence, maintenance, etc.) during the non-building season. If the work was continuous, the total workforce might have been constant, or have varied as men were sent to, or from site in response to various needs. Even if the work was continuous and the size of the labour force constant, the number of men engaged in construction work could have varied as men were moved between construction and welfare.

This flexibility assumes that the labour force was multi-skilled, which is likely. Much of the work was straightforward, and most of the legionaries would have had skills which were transferable. Inevitably though, there would have been some highly skilled workmen (e.g. some of the carpenters), but they could have initially supervised the setting up of work areas and the production of materials. For example, figure **44** shows that most of the timber buildings were constructed in the last two-thirds of the construction period. In the first third of the construction period most of the carpentry teams could have been engaged in timber-felling and preparation. Similarly the skilled masons could have been setting up and supervising the quarrying of stone and preparation of lime.

It has been suggested here that Inchtuthil could have been built by an on-site workforce of about 880 men (over 1,000 days) or 1,465 men (over 600 days). A much larger workforce would have been relatively less efficient as the duration of many tasks cannot, for example, be halved by doubling the number of men. Nevertheless these figures represent a plausible range only, and the true figures may have fallen outside of that range. There may also have been considerable fluctuation.

Inchtuthil is unusual in having barracks with 14 *contubernia*. If each had the usual eight men, this suggests a century of 112 (instead of the usual notional 80), plus centurion and any non-combatants. Some *contubernia* may have been occupied by only one man (e.g. *optio*?) or had another function, or perhaps this legion was of unusual strength. At 80 per century, two cohorts would have consisted of 960 men, say 972 with centurions. At 112 men per century, two cohorts would have been about 1,356 men. These two cohorts figures (972 and 1,356) are conveniently close to the figures suggested above for the size of the Inchtuthil workforce, and are equally plausible (972 men would have taken 905 days; 1,356 men 649 days).

Organisation of the labour force

We know surprisingly little about how the Roman military worked. Were they efficient? Was the Roman army smoothly-run and highly-organised, or was it bureaucratic and wasteful of resources? How much help came from beyond the legion? Was fortress building always necessary militarily, or was it a political decision, or something to keep the men occupied? Did they build with a sense of urgency and purpose? Were fortresses well-constructed or 'gerry-built'? We cannot answer these questions, but they must be raised — they could have had a fundamental impact on the way the work progressed and the resources required.

While we do not know how the labour-force was organised, supervised, or administered, fragments of rosters and returns from numerous sites (e.g. Vindolanda and the Strobi papyrus) suggest that the legions were administratively highly organised and controlled, and this probably extended to construction work. The military discipline system was probably used for the construction work, but geared to behaviour and productivity rather than to supervision of trades. (It is perhaps unlikely that the skilled masons, carpenters, blacksmiths, etc. were centurions.) Supervision of the trades (i.e. controlling the quality of the work) must have been carried out by men skilled in those trades. This could have been achieved by a ganger or master-and-apprentice type system.

The work may have been allocated to centuries (e.g. one century building a barrack block, perhaps with the centurion allocating labour between the various constructional, associated, welfare, and military tasks), but a more centrally organised system would have been more efficient. The main tasks were probably organised separately (e.g. construction, transport, provision of materials, etc.), under the overall charge of a small team (presumably headed by the Camp Prefect).

We do not know whether the work was organised to try to minimise labour requirements or to minimise the construction period. To some extent the two can be traded off against one another. It is possible that it was organised to reduce the number of highly-skilled specialists (e.g. those tasks with higher skills requirements might have been spread over as long a period as practical). Similarly we do not know whether the building programme was organised to take account of a given number of men, or skilled men, or whether the size of the workforce was determined by other constraints such as the need to build quickly.

Labour variations, extras and inefficiencies

Wastage and debris

We must also allow for wastage of materials and for debris. Clearly there must have been both, and this subsection attempts to estimate their significance. Wastage could have occurred due to over-supply, or to spoilage, breakage or carelessness. A well-organised stock-control system with careful handling could have kept wastage relatively low, but this would have increased labour requirements; if minimising labour or construction time were critical there would have been greater wastage. Other forms of wastage were inevitable no matter how much care and organisation were involved, though some 'waste' might have been used elsewhere. For example, conversion of timber to squared sections involves removing some of the outer material, and, even with careful selection, the timbers available would not have conformed to the lengths actually required. Cleaving timber, which requires good straight-grained timber, is likely to have involved significant wastage of timber. Some of the 'waste' timbers could have been used (e.g. for wedges, or as fuel).

Some estimate of likely timber wastage can be made. If we take 35% wastage for conversion (a traditional figure), and allow 25% for over-length losses and joint-cutting, 10% for breakage and spoilage, 20% for natural defects, and 10% for errors in conversion and carpentry, the total requirement might have been in the order of twice that actually incorporated in the buildings. About 16,200m^3 of timber was incorporated in the fortress buildings, suggesting that perhaps 32,400m^3 was felled, with consequent labour implications.

Apart from breakage, some tile would have been lost due to cutting (e.g. to fit at valleys). Broken tile would probably have been crushed and added to mortar, to improve its performance, so tile wastage can effectively be discounted, though the labour associated with it cannot. The likely amount of breakage depends on the amount of handling. If tiles went from kiln to nearby stockpile (man-carrying) to building-site (man-carrying, pack-animal, or cart), losses could have been minimal. Breakage as low as 1%, which is very conservative, would have produced over 30m^3 of broken tile, and required another 3,700 tiles. If tiles were imported (with lots of transfers and opportunity for accident), or much handled (e.g. due to poor stock-control, or complex transport arrangements) then losses could have been high (even over 10%).

Losses of other materials are likely to have been less significant. The production of mortar ingredients could have been slowed or speeded as necessary (allowing for a long lead-in time for lime), and mixing only done as required. Wastage of high-cost materials (e.g. nails, window-glass, lead) is likely to have been due only to unavoidable accidents.

As much as half of the timber wastage would have been on-site and in stores (wastage due to over-length timbers and jointing, breakage and spoilage, and some of the defects and errors wastage); the rest were converted off-site. How long it would have taken to remove this timber debris is difficult to assess. The on-site debris alone (with no allowance for the spaces between the timber scraps) would have filled over 380,000 baskets. At only five minutes to fill and remove each basket-load, this would have taken in the region of 31,800 man-hours. Much of this might have been carried out by the welfare teams (i.e. collecting fuel).

There would also have been a surplus of sub-soil from the foundation trenches, and small quantities of mortar. The volume of spoil would have been equivalent to the volume of foundation timbers, plus a bulking allowance, about 920m^3 (66,000 basket-loads). If this were dumped on the counter-scarp bank (allowing 4 minutes to load and tip, and an average round-trip of 270m), it would have taken about 4,400 man-hours to remove. Alternatively, some spoil might have been used for nearby street-surfacing. Other debris would have been relatively minor. If removing debris from each building took on average one man half-a-day, this would have taken about 700 man-hours.

Variations to lifting

The labour work-rates allow for lifting materials, from ground-level or working-trestles, to their fixing position. During the timber-phase, simple lifting gear (pulleys and ropes, and simple cranes) was probably used because of the relative lightness of most components, and the high cost of provision. It is difficult to assess the significance of lifting gear on man-hours, particularly as the numbers of men for a given task is likely to be reduced but the duration of the task increased. The awkwardness (size, shape and location of some components) and possible unfamiliarity of the task might have made the work far from efficient. There would also probably have been a relatively high amount of waiting and planning time associated with the lifting and positioning of the larger timbers, but the significance of this can only be guessed at. Much depends on the experience of the men involved, and factors such as the weather. Thus one could argue that more man-hours (relative to the 50kg or 110lb per man basis), or less, were needed for lifting. It is perhaps best to use the figures as calculated, as the assumptions are simple and clear.

How significant is lifting anyway? For structural-frameworks, for example, place and fix accounted for about 35% of the tasks, but lifting was only part of this place and fix which includes carrying the materials from the building's preparation area to the fixing location, lifting (often lifting gear would not have been appropriate), and fixing. The amount of lifting varied from building to building, particularly with variations in the size of large timbers and the eaves-heights. For the majority of a fortress's timber buildings the lifting element accounted for less than 10% of the total labour required (about 16% of the total labour for Inchtuthil's tribune's house I, but only 6% for the simpler and lower barracks; barracks accounted for about 50% of the labour required to build the fortress buildings). Thus doubling or halving, say, the lifting component of the figures would not have a major influence on the total labour requirement.

Variations to work-rates

Small variations to one of the variables used in the calculations could have marked effects on the totals. This and the essential conjectural nature of the assumptions about the construction are the main reasons why the figures calculated can only be regarded as indicators of the likely scale of magnitude of the task. Clearly some rates are more significant than others, where the rate is relatively high (e.g. roof-truss carpentry), or frequently repeated (e.g. turf-working), or both (e.g. man-carrying).

Carpentry took almost 43 man-hours per truss, but as each joint took two men the duration of the task was only 21 hours and 20 minutes. The 2,555 trusses would have taken about 110,000 man-hours to prepare (excluding any extra handling). The most time-consuming joint was the rafter tenon (10 hours per joint; 20 hours per truss). If this time were reduced by, say, one hour per joint, this would reduce the total truss carpentry time by 5,110 man-hours (5%), but the total construction time for all fortress timber buildings by less than 0.5%. A rate reduction of 10% for all carpentry would reduce the total time for constructing all buildings by only 1%. Even halving these rates, which is not credible, would only reduce overall labour for the fortress timber buildings by about 5%.

The rampart turf-working was calculated at about 429,000 man-hours (469,000 with team inefficiencies) and involved cutting, loading, moving, and placing almost 938,500 turfs. Relatively small adjustments to the rates would therefore make a significant difference to the labour total. There is reasonable evidence for the turf-cutting rate, and a reduction below, say, eight minutes seems unlikely. Loading could hardly have taken less than two minutes, and the transporting rate seems firm. Unloading and placing might be pared to, say, four minutes. Ignoring team-working considerations, this would reduce the turf-working total man-hours by about 9% (about 8% for all the rampart work), which is significant, though not in terms of constructing the whole of the early timber-phase. However, it could also be argued that the rates are too low: they assume, for example, that reasonable turf was available, and nearby, and without the need for selection or disposal of poorer turf, and that the work proceeded smoothly and was well organised.

The third example is the man-carrying rate. The rate is 1m every 1.3 seconds (2.7km/hr). In practice the rate of travel would have varied to take account of the weight or awkwardness of the load, the distance, the ground conditions, weather, fatigue, urgency of the task, and a variety of other unknowable factors. Inchtuthil's storage area was about 660m from the farthest barrack (the round-trip taking almost 30 minutes). The structural framework timbers for this barrack would have required about 1,800 man-trips, taking 887 man-hours. A reduction or increase in the rate of about 10% (+/- 89 man-hours) seems a relatively large variation, but for all the barracks (+/- 89 man-hours x 66 = 5,874 man-hours) it would have affected construction time by less than 1% (and in practice less than this as the other barracks were closer to the Stores). Alternatively, if transport times were doubled (scarcely credible) the total construction time would be increased by less than 20%.

Team-working

Many of the construction tasks could have been carried out, in theory at least, by one-man teams (the number of workmen was, within limits, not critical, and would have allowed some flexibility in the organisation of the workforce and allocation of tasks). It therefore makes sense to describe the construction effort in terms of man-hours, and to divide it up into man-days, and offset man-days against numbers of men in order to assess either the duration of the work, or the size of the labour force. Unfortunately this approach oversimplifies matters: some tasks could not have been carried out by one man (e.g. lifting heavy items), for others the task limits the size of the work-team, and some tasks are critical (i.e. must be done to prevent delays to necessarily subsequent tasks), and some are seasonal (e.g. applying mortar). The supply of materials and equipment, and the balance between skilled and less-skilled labour are also relevant. The size and composition of the labour force, if it were efficiently used, would have varied over time.

Small teams could have been more efficient than individual-working (e.g. combining a skilled man with a less-skilled apprentice or labourer). Large teams would have involved waiting-time where one team or team-member had to wait (seconds, minutes, or longer) for another to complete a task before they themselves could complete theirs. In practice, where there were several people in a team they would not all have been working at the same rate. Some would have worked slower, or would have had enforced rests in order to co-ordinate their tasks. Much of this is inevitable even with careful and responsive organisation.

Teams could have been organised in many ways. For example, one large team might have undertaken the entire on-site building process, from setting-out to finishes, and might have been responsible for supplying locally available materials. Alternatively, teams may have specialised, say, in earth- and turf-working, or carpentry, or tiling. This can affect labour requirements. In theory specialisation should be more efficient as the workmen will be experienced and skilled in their particular tasks. Alternatively, being responsible for the whole building might have improved morale, and decreased waiting time (it might also have increased it). The size of the teams might be relevant here: if teams were large they could have included the requisite number of skilled men, and if small they could have been task-specific.

It would also have been reasonable for a large team to have been responsible for a complete building, dividing the tasks between smaller sub-teams as necessary to facilitate the work and maximise the use of the skills within that team. Could, for example, a century have built a barrack block? Suppose that a century comprised 80 men, and we allow one-third to work on other tasks, and one-third to supply materials, this would leave about 25-30 men for on-site construction work. These must have been subdivided into work-gangs (their size and composition varying as the work progressed). The main building tasks for Inchtuthil's barrack XVII took 7,370 man-hours. We cannot simply divide this up (e.g. 25 men for 37 days) as some tasks require teams of specific numbers of men (e.g. lifting roof-timbers), and some team-sizes are more efficient (e.g. a tiler might work best with two labourers). Also, a balance of skills must be maintained (e.g. a carpenter is not best employed mixing daub, unless there is no carpentry work to hand), some tasks must precede others, and some tasks have effective maximum and minimum team-sizes. While it is unlikely that a fortress was built in the most efficient manner (indeed this would be difficult even with today's computer-planning aids and supply facilities), it is instructive to see, at least crudely, how the man-hours might have translated into numbers of men or task durations.

133

Building barrack XVII involved setting-out (7 man-hours); excavating wall-trenches (255 man-hours); structural wall-framing (1,371 man-hours); structural roof-framing (1,793 man-hours); cladding/infill and roofing (2,742 man-hours); partitions (614 man-hours); openings (63 man-hours); and flooring (25 man-hours). Setting-out was skilled work, excavating and flooring less skilled, and the remainder a combination of both. These tasks are notionally in sequence, but some tasks could have proceeded in parallel, while some must have preceded others.

Figure **48** shows one way of organising the task to balance daily manpower against total duration time. (This excludes collect times, which can be notionally assessed at a further 984 man-hours, some days requiring at least 10 men.) It shows the sequence of tasks and their earliest-start times, and is based on assumed numbers of men per task (assessed to keep task durations relatively short). This shows where the critical tasks lie: work on the roof-framing must wait until at least some of the wallplates are in position. If roof-framing begins after all wall-framing is completed it would be delayed by four days, though this would reduce the number of men needed per day. Another critical point is roof-covering, which cannot start until at least some of the secondary timbers are fixed, which in turn follows on from placing and fixing at least some of the roof-trusses. Wall-cladding and openings have been spread over a long period (i.e. from their earliest starting-time) to minimise the daily manpower requirements.

Increasing the numbers of men engaged in wall-framing (delaying starting roof-framing until the walls are completed) would reduce the daily numbers by 17 men (e.g. Day 8). Also if the numbers of men for excavating and wall-framing were doubled (to halve task duration), the roof-framing could start earlier, but only by one day, and the number of men required would be more consistent over the work period. Also, the numbers of men required for lifting the truss-timbers could have been taken from the collect team, thus evening out daily numbers further. Both these adjustments are shown in figure **49**. Figure **48** shows the number of men needed each day, or part-day. Assuming the remainder of these part-days were wasted, the total man-hours would increase to 7,648 man-hours. The total man-hours, without allowance for teams and dividing the tasks into working days, is 7,370, an increase for team arrangements and working-days of about 4%. This is not a large amount, but must be allowed for over all the labour calculations. (For figure **49** the increase is only 2%.)

Many more variations could be made to even the numbers of men required each day, or to shorten overall duration. Further examples are perhaps futile. The point here is to illustrate the relative complexity of the allocation of men to the tasks, and ordering the sequence of those tasks, in an efficient way. The main conclusion is that the actual man-hours, and task duration, very probably exceeded the theoretical minimum, perhaps significantly. Another purpose of this exercise is to show that certain tasks cannot start before others are completed, and some may start later and not delay overall completion. It also shows that simply doubling the numbers of men does not halve the duration. Figure **50** attempts a theoretical minimum duration: 20 days (21 if the start of the roof-trusses is delayed one day to even labour requirements). The situation is further complicated if we assume that one large team worked on, say, two blocks at once, allowing labour peak-demands to be met on one building by reducing labour on another.

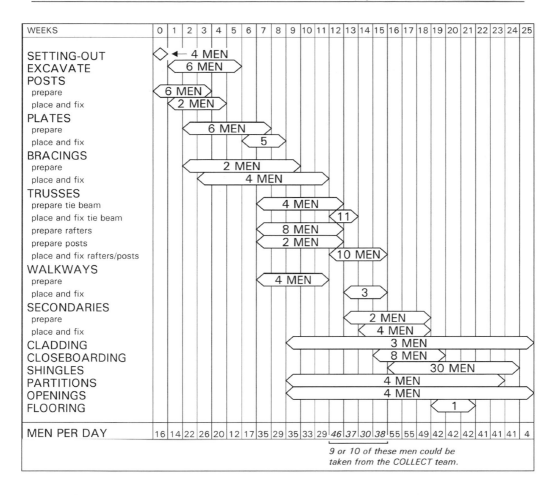

48 Work-programme for a timber barrack — task duration, team-size and earliest start dates

The size of the team is also relevant. The framework of a timber barrack required team-working. All work to the wall-timbers could have been carried out by a team (or teams) of two men. (Collection tasks assume a team of two labourers; for the other tasks at least one man would have been skilled.) Wallplates would have needed four men to move them (if shorter, jointing time would be increased). Roof-framing needed teams of two (carpenter and assistant), with 11 or 12 men for some of the lifting. Thus for a series of sequential construction steps, teams of a variety of sizes and skills levels were needed. This must have involved loss of efficiency as men moved between tasks.

The working day

The effective working day is the amount of the day actually spent in direct construction work, and excludes meal- and rest-breaks, travelling time (e.g. from tent to workplace), and any time needed for other activities and receiving orders. The actual working day would therefore have been longer than the effective working day. An effective notional all-

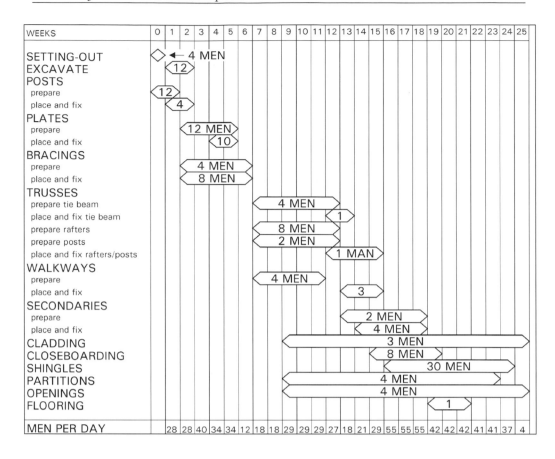

WEEKS	0	1	2	3	4	5	6	7	8	9	10	11	12	13	14	15	16	17	18	19	20	21	22	23	24	25
SETTING-OUT		← 4 MEN																								
EXCAVATE	12																									
POSTS																										
prepare	12																									
place and fix		4																								
PLATES																										
prepare			12 MEN																							
place and fix				10																						
BRACINGS																										
prepare			4 MEN																							
place and fix			8 MEN																							
TRUSSES																										
prepare tie beam							4 MEN																			
place and fix tie beam										1																
prepare rafters							8 MEN																			
prepare posts							2 MEN																			
place and fix rafters/posts										1 MAN																
WALKWAYS																										
prepare							4 MEN																			
place and fix										3																
SECONDARIES																										
prepare										2 MEN																
place and fix										4 MEN																
CLADDING								3 MEN																		
CLOSEBOARDING										8 MEN																
SHINGLES											30 MEN															
PARTITIONS									4 MEN																	
OPENINGS									4 MEN																	
FLOORING																					1					
MEN PER DAY		28	28	40	34	34	12	18	18	29	29	29	27	18	21	29	55	55	55	42	42	42	41	41	37	4

49 Work-programme for a timber barrack — adjustments to show more even daily labour requirements

year average day of eight hours is suggested; this would have been a long day, particularly over a prolonged period. In winter the daylight hours might have been fully used, perhaps with rest-periods taken before dawn and after dusk. Most of the construction tasks would not have been practical by lamp-light, but some welfare tasks (e.g. caring for equipment, or meals) could have been. The length of the day probably varied according to the season, the weather, the stage of the construction work, the availability of materials, and the numbers of skilled and less-skilled workmen available and needed, etc.

It is not reasonable or efficient to work eight hours without a break; this would lead to dehydration, and productivity reduces with task duration. We do not know whether these breaks occurred between tasks, hourly, daily, or whether there were rest-days or parades. Much depends on our assumptions about the hostility of the area and the purpose of the fortress.

It perhaps makes little difference what time the working-day started and finished, and when and how long any breaks were. What is important is how long the men actually worked. It is also reasonable to assume that the builders had some awareness of the effects

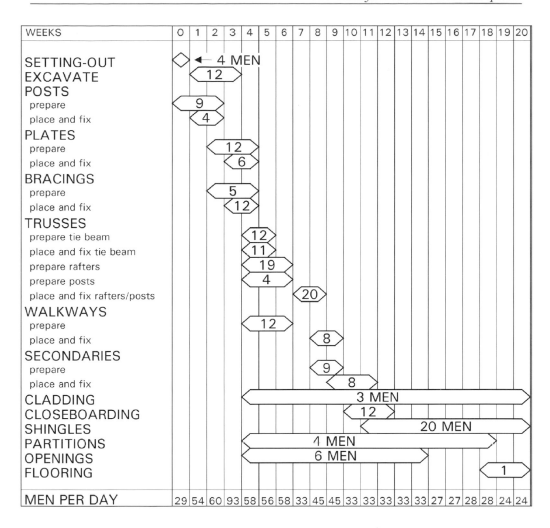

50 Work-programme for a timber barrack — adjustments to minimise completion time

of resting on productivity. If we allow one hour for personal tasks (washing, dressing, latrine visits, etc.), one hour for caring for personal military equipment, one hour for meal-breaks, and half-an-hour for travelling to and from the place of work, there is still time left for other activities (e.g. receiving orders; recreation).

The time of year may have affected the number of men available, and the tasks that could be carried out. Although there were fewer daylight hours in winter, the effective working day need not have dropped below eight hours. It could well have been more in the summer. Perhaps working hours were longer on good days (e.g. ideal weather conditions; long daylight hours, etc.) than on bad days (e.g. frost; snow; heavy rain etc.). These bad days could have functioned as rest-days. On average, time lost during the winter (mostly due to the weather) could have been made up during the summer; thus if we assume year-round working, the eight-hour average working day is reasonable. If work was concentrated in the summer months, the effective working day might have been longer, and if only in the winter, allowance must be made for days lost to bad weather.

Pressures and incentives

Pressures and incentives can only be guessed at. While we can reasonably assume that the work was carried out with military discipline, this does not mean it was necessarily efficiently organised, or carried out by a keen workforce. Alternatively, as the work was presumably for the benefit of the operatives (e.g. providing a less vulnerable position in hostile territory, and improved accommodation) they may have worked with a sense of urgency. There may have been rewards, or punishments, or competition between work-teams. The labour calculations assume a reasonably motivated and efficient workforce, but the work could have been much slower, or more rapid, depending on the actual pressures and incentives. Motivation and productivity may have varied between work-teams (perhaps in response to supervision or location), or over the construction period. Off-site labour might have felt less involved and thus have been less productive.

Organisation, skills and supplies

Organising the supply of materials and equipment, and the appropriately skilled labour, in the right quantities, in the right places, and at the right times is a very complex task. There were conflicting priorities and many variables, some of which were not predictable or controllable. How significant this might have been is impossible to say. Also, we do not know whether they tried to maximise the efficient use of materials, or the use of labour, or to keep the size of the workforce, or the construction period, to the minimum.

Organisational inefficiencies could have occurred due to poor planning of the sequence of the work; incorrect estimation of task-duration; loss or damage to supplies; poor on-site supervision; lack of forward-planning where lead-in times (for supply) are high; or poor estimation of the quantities required or the time needed to source, obtain, make, and move materials, equipment or labour. Poor or delayed communications, and a lack of flexibility or rapid-response to changed circumstances, might also have resulted in inefficiencies.

We do not know whether each legion contained all the relevant specialists and in the required numbers, or what their true level of skill and experience was. It is possible that each legion contained a few highly-skilled men who carried out the more difficult tasks, and supervised a larger group of less-skilled men, who moved from trade to trade as necessary. These men would probably have been less efficient than the skilled and experienced men assumed in the work-rates.

Clearly if materials, equipment, and labour (of suitable type and in the correct quantities) were not in the right place at the right time the work would have been delayed. If materials were delivered to site too much in advance of need they might have been damaged, caused obstructions, or required extra handling. Some inefficiency due to under- or over-supply was, in practical terms, inevitable, particularly where manufacture, extraction, processing, transport times or rates of use could not be accurately predicted.

Discussion

The labour calculations are based on a variety of assumptions, and on minimum inputs or idealised conditions, and must be adjusted (usually upwards) to allow for the possible variations and likely or inevitable extras identified. Some wastage of materials and equipment would have been inevitable, and timber wastage could have doubled the volume of timber required. Man-carrying was the most likely method of transport on-site and locally. Variations to the method of lifting building components were probably not significant, and likely adjustments to the work-rates would not have had a major effect on the overall labour requirement. Team-working, essential for some tasks, would have increased waiting-time and reduced productivity. It is difficult to organise labour efficiently and balance labour numbers against task-duration. The length of the notional effective working day might have varied with the season and the weather, and adverse weather would have affected productivity, as would motivation, the skills of the workforce, and any inefficiencies in the organisation and supervision of the work. The calculated labour figures are thus very much theoretical minimum figures; actual figures would have been higher, in some cases much higher.

Labour requirements to build a fortress

Table F shows that Inchtuthil took 2,440,000 man-hours to build, excluding the later masonry and aqueduct, the on-site support of the builders, and production of building materials, equipment, food and fodder, and transporting them to site. This total of almost 2.5 million man-hours for the early timber-phase works may appear a tremendous amount, but it is only the equivalent of, say, 1,000 men working for 305 eight-hour days. The fortress could have been fully occupied once these early works were completed, and the later timber-phase masonry would have added to the comfort of the fortress occupants (particularly the legate, if he was present during the early construction period).

As might be expected, the fortress buildings and defences accounted for the majority of the effort (nearly 93%). However, the balance of that effort may not be as expected: the timber buildings accounted for a massive 47% of the total constructional effort, the turf-rampart only 21%, and the stone defensive-wall a smaller 14%. This is for the early timber-phase work (mostly the timber buildings and defences); if we consider the entire timber-phase (i.e. the timber-phase later masonry too) the situation is different. Of the complete timber-phase, the timber-buildings accounted for only 20% of the labour effort and the stone defensive-wall for 6%; the later masonry accounted for 60% of the entire timber-phase effort.

It is useful to consider how the early timber-phase work was balanced between the various tasks. Firstly the balance between the defences and the interior: the fortress defences (setting-out, clearance, ditch and counter-scarp bank, rampart, gateways, and the stone defensive-wall) required almost 900,000 man-hours. The fortress interior (setting-out, site-clearance, levelling, surfacing, drainage, water-supply, timber buildings, on-site preparation of materials, and early stonework) required a little over 1,360,000 man-hours. The defences thus took almost 40%, and the interior 60%, of the labour for the fortress itself.

Table F Summary of on-site construction labour for a timber-phase fortress

TASK	MAN-HOURS	A% B%	TASK	MAN-HOURS	A% B%
EXTRAMURAL:	40,000	2% <1%	weather-envelope	340,000	
			partitions	85,000	
OFFICERS' COMPOUND:	120,000	5% 2%	openings	70,000	
			flooring	15,000	
			Total:	1,140,000	47% 20%
PRE-CON-STRUCTION			INITIAL MASONARY:		
Setting out	260				
Site clearance	19,000		defences wall	339,000	
Ditch and bank	35,500		other, minor	26,000	
Rampart	504,000		Total:	365,000	15% 6%
Gateways	11,500				
Levelling	50,000		TOTAL	2,440,000	100%
Total:	620,000	26% 10%	(AS BUILT):		(40%)
PREPARATION	8,000	<1%	LATER MASONRY AND AQUEDUCT		
SURFACING	85,000				
DRAINAGE	13,000		Drainage	20,500	
WATER-SUPPLY	22,000		Latrines	4,000	
latrines	25,000		Gateways	50,000	
			Main Bath-House	750,000	
Total:	1,140,000	6% 2%	*Praetorium*	500,000	
			New *principia*	750,000	
TIMBER STRUCTURES			Aqueduct	1,500,000	
			Total:	3,575,000	60%
set out, excavate	32,000				
structural framing	598,000		TOTAL (finished)	6,015,000	100%

Figures are based on Inchtuthil and are rounded for clarity. The A% column shows figures for the buildings and structures actually built when the fortress at Inchtuthil was abandoned; the B% column shows figures for all the buildings and structures, had the fortress been completed and shows the significance of building all the timber-phase masonry buildings and structures. If the 'missing' two granaries and three tribunes' houses were built in timber they would have taken an additional 90,000 man-hours

The balance between fortress and extramural features: the fortress defences and interior features took 2,260,000 man-hours, and all the features outside the fortress 180,000 man-hours (extramural phase 40,500; officers' temporary camp almost 140,000). The external features thus accounted for about 7% of the labour effort.

The balance between timber-work and masonry in the early timber-phase: the timber features took a little over 1,218,000 man-hours, and stonework structures 365,000 man-hours. This is a total of almost 1,583,000 man-hours, about 65% of the total construction labour. The timber features required much more labour than the masonry features, accounting for about 77% of the total for timber and early masonry.

The balance between what had been completed at Inchtuthil and what was incomplete: a total of 2,075,000 man-hours would have been required to build the later masonry buildings and drains. The aqueduct would have taken in the order of 1,500,000 man-hours. There would perhaps have been two more timber granaries and three more timber tribune's houses, taking a further 90,000 man-hours (alternatively these 'missing' buildings may not have been built until the masonry phase). Thus the buildings and features planned for but not significantly begun would have taken 3,575,000 man-hours, 3,665,000 man-hours if the extra granaries and tribunes' houses are included. This compares with 2,440,000 man-hours for the buildings and features that had been built. On this basis one could argue that, although perhaps habitable when abandoned, Inchtuthil's timber-phase was, in labour terms, not even half-built.

The balance between skilled and less-skilled labour: it is difficult to draw a line between what was skilled work and what was not as most labouring tasks require some experience, knowledge and ability, and many skills can be very quickly acquired. Any division between skilled and less-skilled is thus somewhat arbitrary, but is useful because it can indicate the relative need for specialists, and how this balance changed over the construction period, an important consideration when the work was planned. Supervisory work, organisation and planning are obviously skilled tasks, as are setting-out, carpentry and masonry-work, and the remainder less-skilled. Overall, about one-third of the on-site construction labour was skilled, but the proportion varied significantly depending on the stage of the construction, with very few skilled men needed for the initial works, and many more (about 50%) for the construction of the buildings. 4% of the extramural work was skilled, compared with 19% for the officers' temporary camp, 2% for clearance, rampart and ditch, and levelling, 100% for on-site preparation of materials, 8% for surfacing, water-supply and drainage, and 50% for timber buildings and masonry.

The 2.44 million man-hours represents the labour only of those on-site and directly engaged in the construction work. (Other necessary labour, both on- and off-site, is discussed in chapters 7 and 8.) It is based on a theoretical reconstruction of a timber-phase fortress, which, although conjectural, is reasonable. It assumes a relatively simple and unelaborate design, and an efficient construction process, with no delays or inefficiencies, an experienced and motivated workforce, and an ideal construction-programme. In reality such an ideal situation is very unlikely and the calculated labour figure is therefore very much a theoretical minimum.

10 Conclusions

We have identified the likely type and quantity of materials and labour needed to build a timber-phase Roman fortress. This illuminates much about the construction and character of a fortress, the supply process and military organisation, economic activity, and the condition of the surrounding region.

The materials and labour required to build a fortress

The likely building materials, construction, and the three-dimensional shape of the buildings have been assessed from excavation evidence, Roman texts and finds, traditional building practice, and pragmatism about the building process. The amount of labour required has been calculated using these reconstructions, and identifying each constructional step in the erection of each building. The numbers of men required for each step, and whether skilled or less-skilled, have also been assessed. The labour requirement, expressed in terms of man-hours, has been calculated using work-rates based largely on pre-mechanisation estimators' handbooks, and experimental archaeology. The simplest reasonable material, or most straightforward construction method has been assumed, and critical and non-critical options have been identified. The resultant totals are theoretical minima; in practice the quantity of materials and labour are likely to have been much greater. Necessary non-constructional on-site labour (e.g. for provision of materials, welfare; military tasks) has also been assessed, and other more remote labour requirements (e.g. producing the grain to feed the workforce) identified.

Materials

Table G summarises the main materials needed for a timber-phase fortress (further details can be found in Shirley, 2000.) About 16,200m³ of main-timbers were required (i.e. roof- and wall-framing, and granary floors). Of these the roof truss-timbers accounted for about half of all roof-timbers and about a quarter of all the main-timbers. The roofs were covered with 366,000 *tegulae*, 375,000 *imbrices* and 776,000 shingles, weighing about 4,800 tonnes. (This assumes that the centurions' quarters were tiled; if they were shingled the figures would be very different at 227,000, 234,000, and 965,000.) These roof-coverings and main-timbers would have weighed about 21,600 tonnes. The walls also needed 1,100-3,700m³ of wall-cladding timbers and/or 17,300m³ of wall-infill. 73,200 nails or pegs would have been needed to fix *tegulae*, 776,000 to single-fix shingles, and 706,000 for external cladding. How these materials were distributed between the buildings is shown in figure **51**.

Table G Summary of main materials for a timber-phase fortress

MATERIAL	QTY	TON	MATERIAL	QTY	TON
INITIAL WORKS:			LATER MASONRY:		
main timbers	16,200m³	16,900	main timbers	2,500m³	2,608
external cladding	1,100m³	1,150	*tegulae*	165,000	990
defences timbers	750m³	780	*imbrices*	173,000	433
tegulae	366,000	2,200	stone	28,500m³	68,400
imbrices	375,000	940	sand (masonry)	10,800m³	17,280
shingles	776,000	1,090	lime (masonry)	3,600m³	8,640
wall stone	9,800m³	23,520	water (mortar)	4,350m³	4,350
other stone	550m³	1,320	water (lime slaking)	5,350m³	5,350
sand (masonry)	2,900m³	4,640	nails (tiles)	33,000	<1
sand (roofs, render)	1,900m³	3,040			
gravel (streets)	7,300m³	13,800			
gravel (berm)	1,600m³	3,020			
lime (masonry)	1,000m³	2,400			
lime (roofs, render)	630m³	1,510			
water (mortar)					
daub	3,850m³	7,660			
wattles	50m³	50			
nails (tiles)	73,200	6			
nails (shingles)	776,000	3			
nails (ext cladding)	706,000	3			
rampart turfs	19,000m³				
rampart earth-fill	9,500m³				

Figures are based on Inchtuthil, and are rounded for clarity. If the 'missing' two granaries and three tribunes' houses had been built they would have increased the main-timbers for the initial work by 7% (1,200 tonnes) and tiling by 14% (430 tonnes). Figures for Later Masonry exclude finishes

Different roof-shapes, at different pitches, have different roof-slope and wall areas, and thus require different amounts of framing-timbers and enclosing materials. It has been shown that roof-shape and verge-overhangs are not very significant influences, but roof-pitch and eaves-overhangs can be. Some fortress timber buildings were probably tiled and the rest shingled. If all were tiled, about 925,000 *tegulae* and 957,000 *imbrices*, and over 180,000 nails/pegs would have been needed, but if all were shingled nearly 3 million shingles (plus 3 or 6 million nails/pegs) would have been needed. If all roofs were tiled, more roof-framing timbers would have been needed (increased from about 8,000m³ to nearly 10,400m³), or if all shingled, reduced to about 6,200m³. Suspended-timber flooring

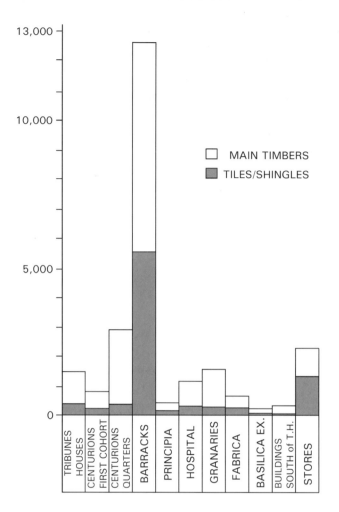

51 Weight (tonnes) of main timbers and tiles/shingles for a fortress's timber buildings

would have increased the required quantities of main-timbers by about 17%, with 10 nails/pegs per m² of ground-plan area.

Wall-posts accounted for 70% of external and structural-partition timbers (about 20% of all main-timbers), and bracings/struts and wallplates accounted for about 15% of wall-timbers each. Non-structural partitions accounted for about 6% of main-timbers, though some buildings had none (granaries), and barracks inevitably had a high proportion (16%). If all the buildings were externally clad this would have needed about 1,100m³ of timber, and internal walls plus the internal-faces of external walls a further 2,600m³ of cladding. Alternatively about 9,350m³ of wattle-and-daub would have been needed to infill all walls, plus any over-rendering. As walls may have been clad (single- or double-skinned) and/or infilled, these figures are partly cumulative. Flooring has been excluded from these main-timber totals (as its existence and form is unclear) except in the granaries. These must have had substantial floors, accounting for about 40% of the granary main-timbers.

It is not possible to say whether the nails found at Inchtuthil were, in terms of numbers, sizes and weights, representative of the nails actually used there. Very large nails may have been removed for recycling, and it is possible that no nails were used there (the nail hoard could have been scrap for recycling). It is more likely that both nails and oak-pegs were used. Nails could have been used to fix *tegulae* (73,200, if one-fifth were nailed), shingles (776,000), and external cladding (706,000). These uses represent 86%, 102%, and 92% of the hoard of nails of appropriate size, and would have weighed about 6.5 tonnes. Nails might also have been used to fix internal cladding (requiring 533,000-1.7 million), roof-closeboarding and granary floorboarding, to peg carpentry-joints (instead of oak-pegs), and are probable for fixing door-hinges etc. Oak-pegs would have been massively cheaper than nails (in terms of resources, labour inputs for production and transportation, and lead-in times), and would have been more adaptable, would not have split or stained the timbers, but would have taken longer to fix.

The barracks would have accounted for the majority of the building materials (about 42% of main-timbers, 6,840m³), and the centurions' quarters for about 19%. These were thus the most important buildings in terms of materials. (The senior officers' houses accounted for only 10%, the granaries 8%, and the *principia* and *fabrica* each less than 4% of all main-timbers.) These calculations assume a very conservative 20° roof-pitch for the barracks; a more reasonable 30° pitch would have needed about 5% extra main-timbers and shingles. Adding 100mm to barrack eaves-heights would increase barrack main-timber requirements by only 1%, and wall-cladding by about 3%. If the barracks had tiled roofs, each block would have needed 40m³ more roof-timber (about 21m³ more timber after the volume of shingles has been omitted). This is an extra 1,370m³ (1,430 tonnes) for all the barracks, an increase of over 40%. In addition there would have been around 458,000 *tegulae*, 468,000 *imbrices*, and 834m³ mortar. These tiles would have weighed about 2,575 tonnes more than shingles.

Labour

Labour requirements for the building work for a timber-phase fortress are summarised in **Table H**, and in **Tables E** and **F**. The extramural features required about 40,000 man-hours and Inchtuthils' officers' temporary camp 120,000; the pre-construction work 620,000 (of this the rampart took 504,000 man-hours); on-site preparation of materials 8,000; drainage, surfacing and water-supply about 145,000; the timber structures 1,140,000 (600,000 for their structural frames); and the initial masonry 365,000 man-hours (including 339,000 for the defensive-wall). This is a total of 2,440,000 man-hours. Figure **52** shows how the labour for the timber buildings was divided between the main construction tasks. 60% of the labour required for the fortress itself was expended on the interior buildings and features, and 40% on the defences. About one-third of the labour was skilled, though little of this was highly skilled work. The later masonry and aqueduct, presumed to have been built as soon as the timber buildings were complete, would have taken another 3,575,000 man-hours. This is a total of just over 6,000,000 man-hours for on-site construction work.

Other essential labour requirements are summarised in **Table E**. 2,000,000 man-hours were needed for additional labour (including 530,000 for guarding and protection, 320,000 for military training, and 210,000 for organisation, administration, and supervision); 1,279,000 for provision of building materials locally (including 554,000 for

Table H Summary of labour for a timber-phase fortress

TASK	MAN-HOURS
INITIAL WORKS:	
ON-SITE CONSTRUCTION	2,440,000
SUPPORT	
additional labour	2,000,000
provision of materials	1,280,000
transport of materials	660,000
transport food/fodder	666,000
LATER MASONRY WORKS AND AQUEDUCT	
ON-SITE CONSTRUCTION	3,575,000
SUPPORT	
additional labour	3,575,000
provision of materials	730,000
transport of materials	980,000
transport food/fodder	570,000
TOTAL LABOUR	
Initial work	7,046,000
Later works	9,430,000
TOTAL (rounded)	16,500,000

Figures are based on Inchtuthil, and are rounded for clarity. ON-SITE CONSTRUCTION is the actual building work on site, and includes the turf-rampart (504,000 man-hours), stone defensive-wall (339,000 man-hours) and timber-buildings (1,140,000 man-hours). ADDITIONAL LABOUR includes organisation, military tasks, and welfare of men and animals. STANDARDS: these figures are for basic buildings, and exclude fittings and decorative finishes. STONE QUARRYING: The rate is very conservative, it could plausibly have been up to almost ten times greater

timber-felling and preparation); 660,000 man-hours to transport these materials, and 666,000 man-hours to transport food/fodder/water. Non-constructional labour to support the later masonry (mostly the principal buildings) and aqueduct amounted to a further 5,855,000 man-hours. This is a total of 10,460,000 man-hours for essential site-based labour not directly involved in building work.

Thus the on-site construction (6 million man-hours) and support labour ($10\frac{1}{2}$ million man-hours) to build a timber-phase fortress has been calculated at almost $16\frac{1}{2}$ million (16,476,000) man-hours. This excludes any inefficiencies, many of which would have been inevitable, and the labour-intensive provision of iron-billets, glass, foodstuffs and fodder, tools and equipment, and their transportation to site.

Rebuilding in masonry

Any assessment of the materials and labour needed for rebuilding a fortress in masonry is much more tentative because of the very much wider range of material and design options, and the unknown timescale for the work. Approximations suggest that masonry fortress buildings, of conservative design, would have taken at least 3.3 million man-hours, not allowing for demolition of the timber buildings, site preparation, hypocausts and associated features, and decorative finishes and fittings. These, and a higher standard of design and finish, could easily have doubled the requirement for on-site construction labour. To this must be added provision of a water-supply pipework system, and upgraded provision and specification of drainage, streets and courtyards. This excludes the provision and transport of materials, and on-site non-constructional labour, both of which are likely to have taken significantly longer than the building work itself. It also excludes ongoing maintenance. In practice this rebuilding is likely to have been spread over several years, but it represents a very considerable investment of resources.

The construction period for a timber-phase fortress would have been much greater than the calculations suggest, unless the fortress builders could draw on stockpiles of materials with long lead-in times (e.g. iron-billets, glass). Where a necessarily lengthy masonry-rebuilding programme was in hand, it would have been practical (though not necessarily efficient) for the fortress builders to organise tasks with long lead-in times, such as extraction and processing of iron-ore. It is also likely that they were directly involved in the extraction of stone (with associated road-building between quarry and site) and building and running brick-and-tile kilns. Specialist finishes (e.g. marble veneers) are more likely to have been bought in, and perhaps also some of the specialist labour.

Inchtuthil

Inchtuthil is important because it is the only fortress where the complete ground-plan is known. This, plus the known occupation period and the timber construction, has allowed detailed calculation of the types and amounts of building materials and labour required to build a timber-phase fortress.

The on-site construction work at Inchtuthil would have taken about 2.5 million man-hours, and necessary on-site support labour approximately 4.6 million man-hours. These figures are very much theoretical minima. Had the fortress been completed, at least a further 3.6 million man-hours would have been necessary for on-site construction, and almost 5.9 million for on-site support. This suggests that the complete fortress would have

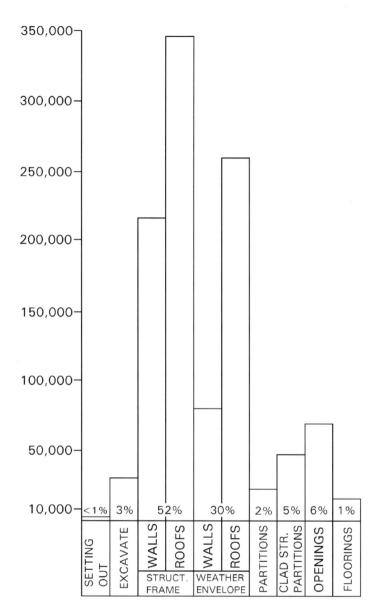

52 The labour requirements for the main constructional tasks for a fortress's timber buildings

required, for on-site construction and support labour, about 16.5 million man-hours. Although no two fortresses have the same layout, Inchtuthil conforms broadly with the usual arrangement, so these figures are roughly transferable to other fortresses.

The extramural features and officers' temporary camp at Inchtuthil were relatively insignificant in terms of labour requirements (about 5% and 2% respectively of the on-site constructional effort). However, they are interesting because we do not have firm evidence of their purpose. If the officers' temporary camp was a temporary camp for senior offices and their guard, its buildings need not have been so elaborate, or have included the (unused) small bathhouse. (They were perhaps intended for senior officers, and later for the legate, until their fortress residences were built.) The labour camps may not have housed the construction force, and camp I may not have housed men at all, and a defensive explanation for the outer masking earthwork and western *vallum* is not entirely satisfactory. Understanding their purposes would shed light on the processes and progress of the construction of the whole fortress, and the nature of the occupying force.

The layout of the fortress also poses questions. Why had construction of the other two granaries not been begun? Were barracks A and B (next to the first cohort's) and their adjacent *tabernae* for cavalry? Where were the stables? (The lack of solid flooring and drainage provision suggests that *tabernae* were probably not stables.) The pack- and draught-animals were, presumably, corralled outside the fortress, but where? Why did the barracks have so many *contubernia* (14 instead of the more usual 10-13)? Where was the parade ground; had it been built? What was the *basilica exercitatoria* used for? If the fortress had been completed, would the open-spaces have been infilled, and with what?

One of the aims of this book has been to shed some light on the processes of building. Some of these processes are unique to a military fortress (e.g. layout, building design) and to a frontier zone (e.g. supply logistics), but some are relevant to the building of any timber or other structure (e.g. planning, organisation of the workforce, the progress of the work stages). It is all too easy to see fortress building in semi-abstract terms (e.g. as an example of military planning, or Roman might, or part of a process of military conquest) and overlook the practicalities of building. These include the effects of bad weather on the progress of the work, and on the working conditions of the men, the difficulties of matching the supply of materials, and of men with the necessary skills, to the various and perhaps conflicting day-to-day requirements. These are essentially unknowable, but inevitable, matters.

The fortress itself can tell us something about the possible building processes; some work must have preceded other work (either essentially, or because some tasks are critical for completion). The relative labour requirements of some tasks may suggest possible work programmes. This is of course all very speculative, but with some foundation. Inchtuthil had to be built from raw materials, and this involved a very considerable effort in terms of basic physical tasks (e.g. felling trees and preparing timber, excavating earth, digging latrines, man-carrying of baskets and timbers, etc.) by men who, for much of the time were living in cramped conditions in leather tents, without bathing facilities or even a piped water-supply, and perhaps under the constant threat of attack.

In one sense, because Inchtuthil was not finished, it did not function fully. Nevertheless it was partially occupied, and some streets had become rutted. It also functioned in the sense of having achieved the majority of its layout, and becoming a defended site. What is of interest here is how it might have functioned had it been completed and occupied.

Buildings of timber can be superior to those of stone in terms of warmth, and lack of condensation. They may have been crudely built and draughty, or well-built and comfortable. They could have had reasonably good natural lighting, and if the walls had two-skin construction, and floors were timbered, could have been relatively warm and draught-free. Surfaced streets, accessways and courtyards, and adequate drainage-channels, could have ensured a well-drained and mud-free environment.

Green timber would have warped as it seasoned and responded to seasonal changes in moisture content, and this would inevitably have led to movement. Unless carpentry joints were inadequate, or not re-wedged where necessary, this need not have been of structural significance. These movements would have caused small gaps and cracks in wall and roof surfaces, though regular routine maintenance could have minimised draughts and water ingress. The mortar on the roofs, particularly at valleys, would also have deteriorated (because of movement and weathering), and have required regular maintenance to prevent water ingress and consequential timber decay.

The buildings could have been relatively luxurious (the hypocausts suggest that parts of some were), or very basic, as places to live and work in. Neither do we know the standard of repair and maintenance. An army used to living at least part of the year in tents might be expected to be hardy (though there are literary references suggesting this was not always so), and this might support the view that these buildings would be basic. Alternatively centurions, and to a lesser extent all Roman citizens, were used to a relatively luxurious standard of living as civilians, and this might suggest more sophisticated fortress buildings (there is evidence of painted wall-plaster, drainage, and solid-flooring in stone-built barrack blocks).

Perhaps the most likely possibility for Inchtuthil, at least while it was in the initial stages of its timber-phase, was that the buildings were well-built (i.e. structurally sound, with close-fitting components) but of a simple design with little or no internal finishes. Thus they could have been reasonably light, warm and dry, but with rough-timber and render or daub finishes, and rammed-earth flooring.

A comparison between the materials required to build a fortress and a fort is useful to put the fortress-building into context, particularly if the effort of an advance into a new region is considered. Fortresses were not built in isolation, and associated forts may have been built by the same personnel. Inchtuthil was a fortress of nearly 22ha (55 acres); Strageath, a nearby fort of about 1.8ha (4.5 acres). Although there was a difference in scale and function, the difference in the size of the buildings was not of this order. Flavian Strageath would have needed about 1,600m^3 of structural timbers, compared with 16,200m^3 for Inchtuthil. This was one of about 13 forts broadly contemporary with Inchtuthil. Another was Fendoch, which would have required about 1,300m^3 of structural timbers.

It is widely believed that legionaries, not auxiliaries, built forts. It is thus likely that whoever was responsible for Inchtuthil was also responsible for building the associated forts, though auxiliaries may have undertaken other necessary tasks. They would have needed in the region of 20,000m^3 of timber (almost 25% more than Inchtuthil) and about 2.5 million man-hours for on-site construction, and 5.1 million for the necessary support work, say 7.6 million man-hours, plus provision and transport of iron-billets, tools and equipment, foodstuffs and animal fodder to build these forts.

The importance of the scale of supply

When Inchtuthil was built, either during AD 82/83 or 83/84, the army in the northern frontier of Britain was of considerable size. The Roman force at the battle of Mons

Graupius (AD 83 or 84) has been estimated at between about 21,000 and 30,000, though the intended occupying force was probably smaller. During Inchtuthil's construction period its workforce might have been constant or seasonally variable, or varied to suit the constructional tasks. The former seems more plausible, if only because organizationally it is the simplest and the most efficient option. Also, it is difficult to see how a large number of men could have over-wintered there without substantial latrine facilities; perhaps their remains await discovery.

A workforce of around 1,000-1,500 men could have been responsible for building Inchtuthil's associated forts. This is a substantial commitment (7.6 million man-hours, or 960,000 man-days), but in overall military terms not a massive proportion of the total commitment for this campaign. Although it is possible that the size of the on-site construction workforce was constant, it is likely that most of its personnel were not. Building (which involved many different skills) was a form of military training, and a legionary's time would have been allocated between constructional and other necessary tasks, including military training, and guarding and protection of the site and supply routes. Thus some of the overall constructional effort for building Inchtuthil could be regarded as direct military activity (and some of these tasks would have been necessary once the fortress was completed).

Before a fortress was established, the local native population, and the wider region, might have been under considerable pressure from the Romans, with consequent disruption of agriculture and food supplies, and guerrilla-type raiding (e.g. of foraging parties, timber-felling teams, supply routes). But if a fortress was built immediately after a major battle, or in a sparsely populated area, the construction work might not have been disrupted. Thus the initial construction work could have been carried out with considerable or little need for the guarding and protection of sites and supply routes. Thus more, or less, men may have had to be allocated to military tasks rather than directly productive construction work. Guarding and protection at Inchtuthil during the construction was estimated at about 530,000 man-hours (about 8% of the Inchtuthil based labour). Complete omission of guarding and protection is perhaps unlikely, but a significant reduction might be plausible here, allowing more men to engage in construction work, and thus reduce the construction period.

Feeding and equipping four legions at the edge of the Empire (e.g. the campaign that included Inchtuthil) must have required considerable organisation. Fragmentary written records suggest a detailed and comprehensive administration, and we know that the legions included considerable numbers of soldiers with clerical duties. This does not necessarily mean that the organisation was efficient, or that labour or materials and equipment were used economically. However, the rate of the conquest of Britain does suggest that the military were capable of supplying an army in the field, over considerable distances and for a considerable period. Logistics is no simple matter, and an army of this size could not 'live-off-the-land'. Food supplies were essential and several recent studies of logistics show that food and fodder requirements would have been very significant.

Many items of equipment (weaponry, cavalry equipment, domestic items etc.) could not have been provided by the native population (due to their specialist nature or the scale of the demand). They must therefore have been produced for, and probably by, the military. Much of this would be an on-going requirement (e.g. even a garrisoned army would need some regular replacement of equipment), but any equipment lost during campaigning would have to have been made good rapidly. Sim (1994) has shown that a soldier's personal weaponry represented a very considerable investment of resources. All this had to be predicted and organised for.

We do not know how much wastage there was, or how often campaigns or construction work were delayed or endangered by lack of supplies. Tacitus makes no criticism of Agricola's ability to supply his army, and Vegetius implies that the importance of supply was understood and its practice was not a major problem. Much of the organisation might have been based on experience-based rules-of-thumb, but if an army on campaign or a construction workforce were not to be significantly hampered in its actions, there must have been an organisation capable of responding to the unpredictable and the variable.

The effects of building a fortress

The effects of building a fortress, or of rebuilding in stone or brick, would have varied with each fortress depending on its location (the proximity of native and Romanised populations, raw materials, transport routes, etc.) and the length of the construction period. Building a new (timber-phase) fortress in a remote region might have had little economic effect, but the rebuilding of an established fortress, in masonry and with specialised finishes and fittings, particularly in a populated area, could have been a significant economic influence.

Many of the effects of building a fortress were probably unintentional, or not fully understood. Even in sparsely populated areas there must have been some disruption to native landholding, and to trade routes and patterns. Taking vast quantities of raw materials (trees, stone, etc.) need not have had much effect unless we assume a local shortage. Taking large quantities of food and fodder from the local area would have upset established patterns, but these supplies might have been imported by the army, or produced locally by them, thus causing little economic effect locally or elsewhere.

We do not know how large the labour force would have been, but for initial construction or substantial rebuilding, the workforce must, at times, have numbered several hundreds. Except in remote or hostile areas this concentration of relatively affluent people would have been a focus for merchants and service-providers. Indeed most fortresses attracted a settlement.

Where materials came from, and how their supply affected areas remote from the fortress is a matter for speculation. If the items (grain, iron, etc.) were produced entirely by the military, and transported by them, then effects could have been minimal. However, it seems probable that some civilians were involved, whether engaged directly by the army (e.g. to smelt iron, or supplying goods for purchase/taxation/extortion), or indirectly (e.g. providing goods and services for those directly engaged in production and transportation).

A major factor is the lifetime of the fortress. For example, Inchtuthil, built in a remote region and demolished after two or three years, is unlikely to have had major or lasting effects. Here the economic implications could have been relatively limited. The majority of the building materials could have been provided locally, without recourse to purchase or taxation. Providing, or at least transporting, foodstuffs and fodder to site would have been onerous but a concern of the military alone.

It has been assumed that the labour for the initial construction of a fortress (i.e. all of the on-site constructional, and all or most of the support labour) was provided by the legion, and that at least some of the provision (of iron-billets, foodstuffs, fodder, tools and equipment) was under direct military control. The work carried out by the legion at Inchtuthil probably had little or no economic influence. Much of it was cutting down trees, moving earth, and servicing the day-to-day needs of the legion itself. There need have been no local acquisition of materials (by purchase, taxation, extortion, etc.), and thus no stimulus towards a monetary economy, nor the provision of a market. Any manufactured materials (e.g. tiles) were probably made by the workforce themselves, and any local raw materials (e.g. clay and timber) were probably not purchased, and may not have been seen by the native population as resources. Their use need not have affected the local economy.

The army needed feeding wherever it was, and whether it was campaigning, building, or garrisoned. Thus the construction itself was irrelevant, unless foodstuffs were obtained locally from the native population. The latter may have been too few and too much under pressure to have produced a significant surplus, and food and fodder (other than any grazing on uncultivated land) was probably imported, at least during the initial construction period. The economy of the area that produced this food and fodder must, however, have been stimulated, but this might have been the same wherever the workforce was based.

There may have been civilians involved with transportation (e.g. ships, barges, pack-animals), but these were probably not based in the region around the new fortress. Nevertheless the transport requirements (other than those supplied by the legion itself) must have stimulated the economy in some way, whether directly or indirectly. This would have been a relatively short-lived stimulus, unless civilians were regularly used by the army for its supply requirements. It need not have influenced the economy of the areas that the transports travelled through.

Provision of specialist materials, tools and equipment might have been entirely within military control, from extracting iron-ore to transporting finished or semi-finished goods to site. However, some civilian input is possible, either by direct purchase or taxation-in-kind, or by employing civilian labour. These goods and worked raw materials are likely to have been produced at a distance from the fortress, and even if directly under military control, these concentrations of manpower must have provided a market for goods and services. A new fortress could thus have contributed to the continuation of these distant sites and markets. The new fortress's workforce had probably previously been based at an established fortress, where they would have been a market for goods and services. Once they left, this market may have disappeared or been reduced. Thus building new fortresses may also have had some negative economic influence.

Thus much of the activity associated with construction need not have significantly stimulated trade or disrupted existing market networks (i.e. Roman labour utilising otherwise unused and unvalued raw materials, for their own direct consumption, with no monetary exchange or influences on supply and demand). Economic influences are likely, but were probably indirect (e.g. providing or maintaining a market where other soldiers were concentrated, remote from the new fortress, producing basic materials and foodstuffs needed for the army in general). Much of this was not so much related to a particular site as to maintaining the army in Britain.

The requirements for transportation (including the provision of transport equipment, and maintaining routeways), and the supply of tools, construction equipment, and specialist building materials, may have imposed a significant burden on the military, albeit distant from the new fortress. This is particularly so when the requirements of auxiliary forts (and the army elsewhere) are also considered; the military may have had difficulty meeting the demand. This could have had a significant impact, at least during a major campaign, on town-building.

What more could we learn?

This book has centred on fortresses, but the approach to building a fort or small town would have been much the same. The real difference is that a military context simplifies the likely processes and options, and allows the assumption that the workforce were reasonably well disciplined, motivated, and trained, and that construction and supply were probably not delayed for financial reasons. Thus this basic approach could be applied to other sites, including civilian ones.

The excavation of timber structures has improved considerably since Richmond's excavations at Inchtuthil, with awareness of the need to measure and record accurately not just timbers but also post-holes and trenches, and any timber fragments and biological remains. Tool-marks can also indicate the way that timber was worked, and detailed examination of the immediate area might reveal fragments of other building materials, or indicate working areas. There has been regular aerial photography of fortress sites, which can show considerable detail, but limited modern excavation or geophysical surveying. Both could provide much valuable detail about the fortress and the extramural areas, and how they were built and occupied.

At Inchtuthil a detailed excavation of, say, a barrack block (the most important buildings in terms of quantities of materials and labour) would be the most obvious target if a limited excavation was undertaken. This would be of wider relevance, to military and Roman building and the use of fortress buildings. Perhaps more useful in terms of the information that might be revealed would be a remote sensing survey of the fortress and the extramural areas, particularly the labour camps. This might show other hoards of concealed materials, and more evidence of the occupation of the labour camps. It might also be possible to locate the aqueduct, possible nearby furnaces for iron smelting, brick and tile kilns, or confirm that it was not started, and locate the parade ground.

There is also further theoretical work which could be undertaken, including a detailed theoretical investigation of the minimum likely water-supply and drainage (surface and foul) requirements of a fortress, and exploration of ways in which these might have been achieved. Experimental archaeological work on the use of Roman tools in preparing the timbers and forming the carpentry joints; the use of the nails; quarrying stone; and the time taken to produce these tools would be valuable. This could establish a range of work-rates, wear rates for tools, and show the trade-off between time taken and skill and standard of work, and the necessary attendance to assist the skilled men.

More work could also be done on the likely functioning of fortress buildings, for example how variations in the size, shape, and positioning of windows, doors and vents would affect natural lighting and airflow, or assessing how effective braziers might have been. Calculations could be made to show how effective the various wall construction options would have been in terms of insulation values and damp penetration and decay (i.e. comparing the various combinations of single and double-skin wall construction). Work could also be done on the supply of domestic and personal items, other equipment, and decorative finishes. Consideration could also be given as to how the buildings were used (e.g. what were all the *tabernae* for?), and how the fortress buildings and roads might have responded over time to normal use and adverse weather.

This book has emphasised the practicalities of constructing the initial timber-phase of a fortress, and is based on recent work. Detailed work of a similar nature on the practicalities and supply implications of constructing military masonry buildings has to date been limited, but would be very illuminating.

Selected bibliography

A detailed bibliography is included in: Shirley, E.A.M. (2000) 'The Construction of the Roman Legionary Fortress at Inchtuthil', *British Archaeological Reports*, British Series No. 298.

The army, soldiers and equipment

Bishop, M.C. and Coulston, J.C.N. (1993) *Roman Military Equipment*. Batsford.
Davies, R.W. (1989) *Service in the Roman Army*. Edinburgh University Press.
Davies, R.W. (1971) 'The Roman Military Diet', *Britannia* II: 122-42.
Elton, H. (1996) *Frontiers of the Roman Empire*. Batsford.
Holder, P.A. (1982) *The Roman Army in Britain*. Batsford.
Hyland, A. (1990) *Equus: the Horse in the Roman World*. Batsford.
Johnson, A. (1983) *Roman Forts of the First and Second Centuries AD in Britain and the German Provinces*. Adam and Charles Black.
Peddie, J. (1994) *The Roman War Machine*. Alan Sutton.
Watson, G.R. (1969). *The Roman Soldier*. Thames and Hudson.
Webster, G. (1969). *The Roman Imperial Army in the First and Second Centuries AD*. Adam and Charles Black, London.

Military supply and transport

Anderson, J.D. (1992) 'Roman Military Supply in North-East England', *British Archaeological Reports*, British Series, Vol 224, Oxford.
Breeze, D.J. (1986/87) 'The Logistics of Agricola's final campaign', *Talanta*, 18/19, 7-28.
Cotterell, B. and Kamminga, J. (1990) *Mechanics of Pre-Industrial Technology*, Cambridge University Press.
Kendle, R. (1996) 'Transport logistics associated with the building of Hadrian's Wall', *Britannia*, vol. XXVII, 129-52.
Pearson, A. (1995) 'Building Anderitum: The construction of the Roman Saxon Shore Fort at Pevensey', Master's thesis, Dept. Archaeology, University of Reading.
Roth, J. (1991). 'The Logistics of the Roman Army in the Jewish War', PhD thesis, Columbia University.

Fortresses and military buildings

Pitts, L.F. and St Joseph, J.K. (1985) 'Inchtuthil. The Roman Legionary Fortress', *Britannia Monograph*, no.6, Society for the Promotion of Roman Studies.
de la Bedoyere, G. (1991) *The Buildings of Roman Britain*. Batsford.
Gentry, A.P. (1976) 'Roman military stone-built granaries in Britain', *British Archaeology Reports*, British series, vol 32. Oxford.
Davidson, D.P. (1995) 'Military Housing' in Barton, I.M. (ed.) *Roman Domestic Buildings*, University of Exeter.
Manning, W.H. (1975) 'Roman military timber granaries in Britain', *Saalburg Jahrbuch*, vol.32, 105-29.
Rickman, G. (1971) *Roman Granaries and Store Buildings*. Cambridge University Press.
Petrokovits, V.H. von (1975) *Die Innenbauten Romischer Legionslagger Wahrend de Prinzipatszeit*. Westdeutscher Verlag. (Extensively illustrated with fortress and fortress-building plans.)
Zienkiewicz, J.D. (1986). *The Legionary Fortress Baths at Caerleon*. National Museum of Wales and Cadw, Cardiff.

Building

Adam, J.-P. (1994) *Roman Building. Materials and Techniques.* Batsford
Brodribb, G. (1987) *Roman Brick and Tile.* Alan Sutton.
Cleere, H. (1976) 'Some operating parameters for Roman ironworks', *Bulletin of the Institute of Archaeology*, 13: 233-46.
Cleere, H. and Crossley, D. (1985). *The Iron Industry of the Weald*, Leicester University Press, Leicester.
De Laine, J. (1997) 'The Baths of Caracalla', *Journal of Roman Archaeology*, supplementary series no. 25, Rhode Island.
Dix, B. (1982) 'The manufacture of lime and its uses in the Western Roman provinces', *Oxford Journal of Archaeology*, 1(3), 331-45.
Hobley, B. (1971) 'An experimental reconstruction of a Roman military turf rampart', *Roman Frontier Studies* 1967, 21-33.
Peacock, D.P.S. (1982) *Pottery in the Roman World*, Longman Archaeology Series.
Sim, D. (1998) 'Beyond the Bloom: Bloom refining and iron artefact production in the Roman World', *British Archaeological Reports*, S725, Oxford, Archaeopress.
McGrail, S. (ed) (1982) 'Woodworking Techniques Before AD 1500', *British Archaeological Reports*, International series, vol. 129, Oxford.
Mcwhirr, A. (ed.) (1979) 'Roman Brick and Tile', *British Archaeological Reports*, International series, vol.68. Oxford.
White, K. D. (1984). *Greek and Roman Technology*, Thames and Hudson.

Roman texts

Caesar (102-44 BC) *The Conquest of Gaul.* (Describes military practice, including camps, baggage-trains and supplies, and non-combatants.)
Columella (first century AD) *On Agriculture.* (Describes working by artificial light, and work-rates for timber-working and trenching.)
Hygenus (*c.*AD 100) describes the arrangement of a tented camp.
Pliny The Elder (first century AD) *Natural History.* (Describes the care of trees, and felling and qualities of timber.)
Vegetius (late fourth century AD?). *Vegetius: Epitome of Military Science*, Liverpool University Press. Translated by N.P. Milner, 1933. (Describes the arrangement, training, and tactics of the army. It is not a military handbook or true history, and may contain many inaccuracies. It does, however, include a lot of detail, including the age and size of recruits; marching rates and distances; building camps and fortifications; the arrangement of a legion; duties and equipment; supplies; and ships.)
Vitruvius (first century BC) *On Architecture.* (Describes the work of architects including a discussion of building materials (Book II) and finishes (Book VII), the planning of buildings (Book VI), and water-supply (Book VIII). Faventinus (*c.*AD 300) covers similar ground.)
Varro (116-27 BC) *On Agriculture.* (Describes the organisation of an estate. The work covers similar topics to Cato, to which it refers.)
Cato (third/second century BC) *On Agriculture.* (Describes the organisation of an estate, including building, tree-felling, carts, and working conditions.)

Roman writings from military sites
Bowman, A.K. (1994). *Life and Letters on the Roman Frontier: Vindolanda and its people*, British Museum Press, London.
Bowman, A.K. and Thomas, J.D. (1994) *The Vindolanda Writing Tablets*, British Museum.
The Strobi papyrus is translated in: Elton, H. (1996).

Index